The Chiji Guidebook

A Collection of Experiential Activities and Ideas for Using Chiji Cards

Chris Cavert **Steven Simpson**

Published by:

Wood 'N' Barnes Publishing
2309 N. Willow, Bethany, OK 73008
(405) 942-6812

Cover Art by Wood 'N' Barnes Collective
Copy Editing & Layout Design by Ramona Cunningham
Photos by Sam Sikes

Printed in the United States of America
Bethany, Oklahoma
ISBN # 978-1-885473-84-2

For Susana
C.C.

For Manyu and Clare
S.S.

Acknowledgements

We would like to thank several people for their help with this book. Most importantly, thank you to Buzz Bocher and Dan Miller for the creation of Chiji Processing Cards. We hope that the publication of this book will introduce even more people to this excellent teaching tool.

Thank you to Mony Cunningham, our editor. We are fortunate to have a competent editor who not only distinguishes good writing from bad but actually understands the field of experiential education.

Thank you to all of the practitioners who have experimented with Chiji Cards and come up with innovative ways to use them. We especially would like to thank Frank Palmisano Jr., Jen Stanchfield, and Jim Cain for the valuable feedback and ideas they shared during the editing process.

As much as we were able, we acknowledged by name the people who developed new ways to use the cards, but we know that we sometimes missed giving credit where credit was due. If someone was not acknowledged, please know that the omission was not intentional.

Finally, a loving thanks to our families; writing takes time away from them, and we appreciate their continued support of our book projects.

Contents

Preface

There are two groups of people who might take a look at this book. The first will be familiar with Chiji Processing Cards and excited about finding an entire book full of ideas for using them! The second will ask, "What's a Chiji, and why do I need a guidebook for it?" If you are from the first group, you know why you are leafing through this book, so just skip the next two paragraphs and start reading.

For the second group, Chiji Processing Cards were developed as a processing or debriefing tool, a deck of cards actually, used by educators who teach experientially. This includes not only classroom teachers but also nontraditional educators such as wilderness trip leaders, camp counselors, youth group leaders, corporate trainers, group counselors, challenge course facilitators, interpretative naturalists, environmental educators, therapeutic recreation specialists, and so on. From this initial beginning, educators are now using Chiji Cards in a variety of ways.

If you are an experiential educator open to learning new facilitation techniques and curious about how a versatile lightweight prop can liven up your teaching, keep reading. You will discover that you and your program would benefit from Chiji Cards—and from this book as well.

Chris and Steve
September, 2010

Introduction
The Story of Chiji Processing Cards

Experiential educators are innovative tinkerers. Rarely do we take an activity that we've read about in a book and follow the instructions word for word. Neither are we happy with a program idea that we pick up at a workshop until we alter it a bit to fit our agency's specific needs and unique clientele. Before making an activity a part of our educational repertoire, we like to give it a personal touch and make it our own.

This tradition of innovation certainly holds true when it comes to the use of Chiji Processing Cards. Initially developed as a straightforward processing tool to help participants feel comfortable speaking up during processing sessions, variations in the uses of the cards have been popping up since their inception in the mid-1990s. To be honest, the creators of Chiji Processing Cards thought the cards would primarily be popular with novice facilitators uncomfortable with the processing component of an educational program. The creators assumed that, over time, these same facilitators would hone their processing skills and gradually use the cards less and less. This is not what happened. Instead of abandoning the cards after a year or two of experience, seasoned facilitators simply developed additional ways to use them beyond their basic function. This book is an instructional guide describing some of the different ways Chiji Cards* can be used to facilitate key moments during group experiences.

---

* The cards used with this guidebook are sold as Chiji Processing Cards. We will refer to them from this point on as Chiji Cards in order to expand thinking about the cards beyond their use as a processing tool.

A Little Background

*What are Chiji Cards?**

Chiji Cards are a deck of 48 cards with pictures originally designed to spark/enhance discussion during a processing session (see Figure 0.1). When a facilitator asks the group a question, each person chooses a card that symbolizes his or her answer to the question.

Figure 0.1

The images on the cards are used as prompts to help individuals organize their thinking. Rather than having to pull an answer to a question out of thin air, the pictures provide a starting point from which to formulate a response.

For example, each person in a group might be asked to pick a card that represents his or her contribution to a task just completed. One participant might pick the picture of a wrapped gift to point out that his unique talents have yet to be "opened." He admits to the group that he is shy and lacks the confidence to assume a leadership role. If this person really is as shy as he suggests, then the card may help him to talk about his reticence. **It is easier to talk about his card than to talk about himself, even though in talking about the card he is talking about himself.**

---

* Chiji Processing Cards were developed by the staff at the Institute for Experiential Education (www.chiji.com) and are available from many experiential education equipment providers.

Why are they called Chiji Cards?

Two questions often asked are, "How do you pronounce the name of those cards?" and, "What does the word mean?" The pronunciation of chiji is straightforward. Both of the vowels in chiji have a long ē sound, so it is pronounced "chee´ jee."*

The story behind the name "Chiji Cards" began with Buzz Bocher, Dan Miller, and Steve Simpson, co-creators of Chiji Cards, sitting in Steve's living room trying to think of a name for the processing cards they were developing.

"How about 'Turning Point Cards'?" asked Steve. "The cards are supposed to help people apply their experiences to everyday life, maybe even make the experience a turning point. It's not just what they learned by doing the experience. It's also what they are going to do because of the experience."

Dan said, "If we want to stick to experiential-ed jargon, I'd say that we should use the word 'transference' instead of turning point. 'Transference Cards' doesn't sound right though."

"It's better than Turning Point Cards," said Buzz. "Turning point is too grand. People don't have turning points after every little thing they do. Turning points are once- or twice-in-a-lifetime events— changing jobs, moving across the country, getting married. Is there a word for the little twists and turns that happen all of the time?"

Steve said, "I can't think of any single word that means that, at least not in English. Maybe there's a foreign word that gets at it better than English does. Like 'wu li' from the book The *Dancing Wu Li Masters*. I forgot exactly what wu li means, but it has something

---

* "Chee´ jee" is the Western pronunciation, not the Mandarin pronunciation. Mandarin is a tonal language and has four tones. They are 1) steady high, 2) low to high, 3) high to low and back to high, and 4) high to low. In chiji, the *chi* is fourth tone (high to low), and the *ji* is first tone (steady high). In pinyin, the pronunciation of the word would be shown as "chì jī." Most Westerners can't distinguish one tone from another, but to a Mandarin-speaking person, it makes all the difference in the world.

to do with connections between events.* I still have the book somewhere on my shelves. Give me a minute to find it."

Before Steve could get up from the couch to retrieve the book, a voice came from the back of the house, "The word you want is 'chiji.' You aren't talking about wu li. You're talking about chiji." Manyu, Steve's wife, walked down the hallway into the living room. Manyu is from Taiwan, and Mandarin Chinese is her first language. "You are talking about chiji," she said. "It's a Chinese word that means 'key moment.' It's a good word. A chiji moment is a special happening, but it can be either big or small, which seems to be what you are looking for. Its specialness comes from what might happen after the moment, not just the moment itself. The moment could be very big, something that even an unobservant person might notice, but it could also be small and only a person who is paying attention sees it."

"Something that a person like me won't see, you mean," said Steve.

"For you, it depends," Manyu responded. "You'll see details about some ugly little bug or the way ripples form on a lake, then come home and not notice that I moved all the furniture."

"He's an absent-minded professor," said Dan.

"Yes, he is," said Manyu.

"But you love me anyway," said Steve.

"It's endearing and frustrating at the same time. And it means that you'll notice some chiji moments that the rest of us won't, but you'll miss the ones that drop in your lap."

---

* Steve later dug up his copy of *The Dancing Wu Li Masters* by Gary Zukav. "Wu li" is the Mandarin word for physics, which barely applies, but Zukav described a dancing wu li master as an educator who "does not teach, but the student learns." This second meaning or interpretation fit the cards very well. Zukav, G. (2001). *The dancing wu li masters: An overview of the new physics* (pp. 32–35). New York: William and Morrow.

"Is that good or bad?" Steve asked.

"Well, being observant generally is a good thing, but that's not the point," said Manyu. "The important thing is that chiji is not just the event itself. It is what you do with it, too. If you don't even notice a chiji moment, then obviously you have no opportunity to act on it. If you do notice a chiji moment, then you can act on it. That might mean, after thinking about it, you change nothing, which sometimes can be a good decision—or you might change everything."

"And chiji means all of that?" Buzz asked.

"Yes, chiji is the moment, it is the way a person thinks about the moment, and it is the way the person responds to the moment. That might not be the dictionary definition, but that's what Chinese people think when they hear the word. The Chinese character for chi- in the word chiji means 'key,' like unlocking a door. It is not the chi that means inner energy."

"So we're having a chiji moment right now," Buzz said. "If we'd had this conversation somewhere else, or if Manyu hadn't been here, we wouldn't know about chiji. Now we have to decide what to do next."

"That's it then," said Dan. "It's out of our hands. Whether we call them Chiji Cards or call them something else, they really are Chiji Cards."

"No," said Manyu kindly. "If this is a chiji moment, the cards are what you decide they are."

The Chiji Guidebook is Divided Into Two Sections

This guidebook is divided into two sections. The first and shorter section is Theory—processing theory that coincides with the original use of Chiji Cards. While there will be a temptation to skip over the theory and jump directly to the activities, we hope that you give the theory a look. If you have not read much about the educational philosophy behind processing or debriefing, this brief section may provide a rationale for when to use one processing technique over another.

The longer of the two sections is the Activity Guide, 25 different ways to use Chiji Cards. Some activities are designed for processing, meaning they help participants reflect upon an experience or event. Other activities expand the use of the cards beyond reflective processing and help participants to focus on an activity before it begins, to encounter challenge, or to simply have fun. The Activity Guide is divided into six chapters—Processing Activities, Getting-To-Know-You, Frontloading Activities, Object Lessons, Initiative Activities, and Fun With Chiji Cards. Most of the activities we have developed ourselves, but several come directly from other experiential educators who have shared with us their uses of the cards. With so many ways to use a tool that experiential educators already carry around with them, it was time to put these ideas together in a guidebook.

Using image cards is effective because participants can attach their thoughts to an object that can be touched and shown to a group.... When groups use pictures and objects in group discussions, the thoughts, ideas, and connections seem broader and deeper than when using dialogue alone.

—Jennifer Stanchfield

Theory

Chiji Cards and Participant-Directed Processing

Experiential education processing has changed significantly over the last 20 years. Not that long ago, a processing opportunity essentially meant a question-and-answer (Q&A) session following an activity. If processing occurred at all, it was gathering a group of people in a circle and having the facilitator ask a series of questions about a just completed task. Certainly some facilitators were very good at asking the right question at the appropriate moment, but there was little variety in how processing was done. Today most seasoned experiential educators have expanded their processing repertoires to include many different ways to conduct a processing session.* Traditional Q&A remains the mainstay, but it is supplemented with other techniques to help participants reflect on an experience—and Chiji Processing Cards are one small part of this trend.

The introduction to this book mentioned that Chiji Cards were developed with novice experiential educators in mind. While true, that is only part of the story. Certainly one purpose for the cards was to provide an easy, fairly fool-proof technique that encouraged beginners to include processing in their programs. Leading an

---

* Many of these techniques have been compiled into processing guidebooks. Two good examples are Cain, Cummings, and Stanchfield's *A Teachable Moment: A Facilitator's Guide to Activities for Processing, Debriefing, Reviewing, and Reflection* (Kendall/Hunt, 2005) and Sugerman, Doherty, Garvey, and Gass' *Reflective Learning: Theory and Practice* (Kendall/Hunt, 2000).

intelligent Q&A session is an advanced skill, but perhaps first-time facilitators could use a deck of cards to "chiji" a group.

If, however, ease of use was Chiji Cards' only attribute, most facilitators would outgrow them. Even the most patient leader, teacher, or facilitator can hear a participant say, "I picked the light bulb card because I had a good idea" only so many times before the cards fall into disuse and gradually work their way to the bottom of that leader's prop bag. A second motivation behind the further development of Chiji Cards was that they filled a particular niche in the spectrum of processing techniques. **Specifically, Chiji Cards are a tool that shifts some of the responsibility for the success of a processing session from the facilitator to the participants.** This is an important concept and the subject of this chapter.

Processing to Teach Processing

Simpson, Miller, and Bocher (2006) in their book *The Processing Pinnacle*, list 11 reasons for processing with a group (see Figure 1.1). Their purpose for the list was to highlight the fact that there are multiple reasons to process. Not surprisingly, understanding the lessons of the immediate experience topped the list, but it is not the only reason to process. Besides discussing what can be learned from the action component of an experience, processing also is a chance to let participants express their feelings, it is an opportunity to evaluate whether participants have made progress on their predetermined goals, and it is an occasion for the facilitator to teach participants about the importance of reflection and how to process. Most learning experiences in people's lives occur when there is no facilitator looking over their shoulder, so a worthy goal of experiential education is to teach people how to process even when there is no facilitator to guide them.

A basic way of teaching people to process on their own is to have them process frequently while in a facilitated program and trust that this training helps to make reflection a habit. In other words, processing during structured programs may encourage people to reflect more often in everyday life. Obviously this is leaving quite

Eleven reasons for processing with a group, an excerpt from *The Processing Pinnacle* by Simpson, Miller, and Bocher (2006):

- Making sure *all* participants understand the lessons of the action component of the experience.

- Teaching participants about the importance of reflection and teaching them how to process.

- Allowing participants to express both their positive and negative feelings.

- Helping participants to clarify their thoughts by putting those thoughts into words.

- Analyzing the action. This means breaking down an activity into its component parts to better understand why things happened as they did.

- Synthesizing the action. This means trying to take the events of a specific activity and put them in a broader context; i.e., putting the component parts back together following the analysis.

- Helping give the experience permanence. Obviously, some experiences are so dramatic that they will never be forgotten. For other experiences, processing can help to cement the experience in participants' minds.

- Transferring the lessons of the immediate experience to everyday life.

- Evaluating the experience as to whether it accomplished the stated goals and objectives.

- Promoting the value of encouraging participants to fill their lives with a continuous series of educational experiences.

- Bringing closure to an activity.

Figure 1.1

a bit to chance. Does, for example, sitting through a half-dozen Q&A sessions necessarily encourage participants to ask questions of themselves when a facilitator is not there to do the asking?

Educators can be more deliberate in their efforts to teach participants how to process by intentionally sequencing processing activities in a way that progressively puts greater and greater responsibility for processing on the participants. If a leader has a group for an extended period of time, he or she can initially guide participants through carefully orchestrated forms of facilitated reflection. As these participants gain an appreciation of the reflective process, the leader can have the participants assume some of the responsibility for the success of their own processing sessions. When the participants are new to a program and unfamiliar with processing, the facilitator uses processing techniques that are facilitator-centered (i.e., the facilitator pulls most of the strings). When these same participants have done enough processing to understand that an action component of an experience is linked to a period of reflection, the facilitator moves toward processing techniques that shift control of (and responsibility for) processing to the participants.

In terms of sequencing processing techniques, it may be helpful to think of processing as a continuum or spectrum (see Figure 1.2). At one extreme of the spectrum are processing techniques in which the facilitator dictates the way the processing is conducted and even dictates its outcome (e.g., the facilitator intentionally keeps discussion focused solely on the predetermined outcomes). At the other extreme, the facilitator sets aside a block of time for

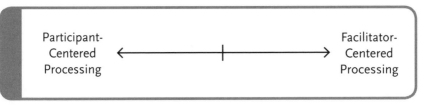

Figure 1.2

processing, but leaves the topics and the methods for processing up to the participants.* When the group needs facilitator guidance to process, the facilitator conducts the processing session. When the group no longer needs help, the facilitator fades into the background and lets the reflection occur naturally. Most processing sessions will be neither as autocratic as the facilitator-controlled extreme, nor as wholly laissez-faire as the participant-controlled extreme, but the balance between facilitator control and participant freedom is not left to chance. Instead it is determined by the choice of the processing technique.

Participant-Directed Processing

The granddaddy of processing techniques is the Socratic Method (i.e., thoughtful Q&A). The key to the Socratic Method is that an educator can lead a student to an insightful answer by asking the right series of questions. Each time a student gives an answer that is incomplete, the educator fleshes out the response by asking follow-up questions. For example,

> Q: What is the difference between true north and magnetic north?
>
> A: I don't know. I never heard of those words before.
>
> Q: A lot of people haven't, but they are important for a map and compass. We'll take the terms one at a time. What do you think true north means?
>
> A: Real. It's the real north.

---

* In *The Processing Pinnacle*, Simpson, Miller, and Bocher (2006) further subdivided both facilitator-directed processing and participated-directed processing to create four categories of processing, but for purposes here, the two extreme delineations will suffice. For readers who would like more on processing theory, we also recommend Luckner and Nadler's *Processing the Experience* (Kendall/Hunt, 1997), Stephen Bacon's *The Conscious Use of Metaphor in Outward Bound* (Colorado Outward Bound School, 1983), and Clifford Knapp's *Lasting Lessons: A Teacher's Guide to Reflecting on Experiences* (ERIC Clearinghouse on Rural Education and Small Schools, 1992).

Q: Yes, but what does that mean?

A: That it's really north, maybe it's pointing to the North Pole or something.

Q: Exactly. Topographical maps are almost always oriented toward true north, meaning that they are pointed toward the North Pole. So what does magnetic north mean?

A: I don't know.

Q: Okay, have you ever heard of the earth's magnetic field?

A: I've heard of it. They are some lines that run up and down on the world, but you can't see them.

Q: That's pretty much right. So if the magnetic field is a bunch of lines that run up and down, then what is magnetic north?

A: Maybe it's where all of these lines are pointing?

Q: Right again. So do you think that true north and magnetic north are pointing to exactly the same place?

A: Yeah, I do, but since you already asked me to tell you the difference, they must not be the same.

Readers can easily imagine how this conversation might progress. The point we want to make is that even though the student was an active participant in the Q&A, the educator in this example maintained control of the processing by determining the follow-up questions. Most facilitators have conducted Q&A sessions where participant responses digress or tend toward the superficial, but the facilitators retained the power to swing the topic of the discussion back to the original purpose and elevate the level of the dialogue by formulating the appropriate follow-up questions. In fact, one of the skills of a talented facilitator is the ability to keep a Q&A session on task.

Eventually, however, participants come to understand what processing is supposed to accomplish—and when this occurs, the facilitator may want to turn responsibility for the processing over to the participants. This will allow the participants to determine the direction of the processing, and it will aid participants in developing their personal processing skills. Processing techniques that give participants such freedom are sometimes called participant-directed processing (PDP). Most of the traditional uses of Chiji Cards can be described as PDP (see Figure 1.3).

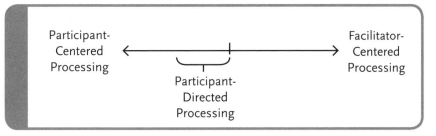

Figure 1.3

For example, Activity #5 in this book is called When Do We Get to Ask the Questions? It is an activity where the participants, rather than the facilitator, ask the processing questions. Use of this activity requires a facilitator leap of faith. Asking the questions has traditionally been one of the ways that facilitators control the direction of the discussion. Handing the question asking over to the participants should not be taken lightly. It definitely should not be done simply as a way to add variety to the processing. In When Do We Get to Ask the Questions?, facilitators intentionally step out of the leader role because they believe that the group is ready to determine the direction of the processing on its own. The content of the discussion is determined by the participants, not the facilitator. In fact, the topics of discussion may not be those that the facilitator would have chosen; if, however, the participants are mature, engaged, and reflective, they are capable of creating their own path during processing.

This participant freedom is the essence of participant-directed processing. The facilitator 1) still makes sure that processing occurs and 2) usually chooses the processing technique to be used, but 3) allows the participants to determine the topics and the direction of discussion.

Two Kinds of Sequencing

We use the term "sequencing" to point out that processing activities should not be used randomly, but in a particular order as participants gradually are able to assume greater responsibility in the success of processing sessions. This, however, is not the usual way that sequencing is used in terms of processing—and it is important to understand both forms of sequencing.

The second, and more common, use of the term is in reference to sequencing processing questions. When a facilitator is using traditional Q&A, it is vital that he or she ask questions in a specific order. Too often, for example, the first question to come out of a facilitator's mouth is, "So how did you feel about the last activity?" The result can be dead silence among the participants, because this is a deceptively difficult question. First of all, participants don't always know their feelings or, if they do know them, are not comfortable expressing them. Secondly, the question is vague. Participants may not know what the leader is looking for. The facilitator may not even know what he or she is looking for. Feelings is an important topic, but one that should be introduced later in the sequence. Putting good questions in the right order is almost as important as identifying the good questions.

There are no hard and fast rules for sequencing processing questions, but as Sugerman, et al. (2000) pointed out, the purpose is to progress from the concrete to the abstract, from the easy questions to the more difficult.* One example of sequencing is shown here. It is a four-step sequence of factual questions followed by feeling questions followed by analysis/synthesis questions followed by transference questions.

Factual questions are simply questions that reconstruct the activity just completed. Examples are "Can someone remind all of us what the stated purpose of the last activity was?" and "We did three activities this morning. What were they in the order that we did them?" Sometimes factual questions serve a specific purpose, although they sometimes are just simple, nonthreatening questions to get the discussion started.

Feelings questions are just that, questions that get to the feelings of the group or of individuals within the group. Sometimes a facilitator may just ask the vague question, "So how did you feel about the last activity?" More often the questions are a bit more focused. For example, "For the first time this afternoon, I sensed a little frustration in the group. By a raise of hands, how many people felt frustrated?" Then after a raise of hands, the facilitator follows up with, "Would anyone be willing to say why they were frustrated?" "Is frustration okay? Why or why not?"

Analysis questions/synthesis questions are drawing out the lessons of the experiences. Stated most simply, analysis is breaking down the activity into its component parts; synthesis is putting the parts back together into a coherent whole. Examples of analysis/synthesis questions include, "Carrie just said that she was frustrated because she tried to speak up three different times, and not a single person seemed to be listening. Can anyone explain why that was? If we agree that listening to everyone is important, what are two specific things that we can do to make sure that less-assertive people also get heard?"

---

* Sugerman, D. A., Doherty, K. L., Garvey, D., and Gass, M. (2000). *Reflective learning: Theory and practice* (pp. 12–16). Dubuque, IA: Kendall/Hunt. As facilitators hone their skills, we suggest that they look at the sequencing of questions more carefully. In addition to Sugerman et al., other good sources about sequencing questions are Quinsland, L. K., & Van Ginkel, A. (1984). How to process experience. *Journal of Experiential Education, 7(2)*, 8–13, Hammel, H. (1986). How to design a debriefing session. *Journal of Experiential Education, 9(3)*, 20–25, and Knapp, C. E. (1992). *Lasting lessons: A teacher's guide to reflecting on experience.* Charleston, WV: ERIC Clearinghouse on Rural Education and Small Schools.

Transference questions are taking the facilitated experience and applying it to everyday life. Questions might be, "I heard people joking at least three different times that you are cooperating so much better today than you do at work. Give me three reasons why you think that is so," followed by, "Okay, evocative comments. What are some very concrete, specific things that you as a group could do to carry this sense of cooperation back to the job? That's what you are here for, after all." An excellent closing statement, which also is transference, is, "Okay, before we finish up and go our separate ways, I'd like to go around the circle and have each person state one thing, just one thing, that you learned today that you can commit to using in the future."

Whether sequencing processing activities or sequencing processing questions, the overall purpose is basically the same—helping participants to process successfully by presenting them with the next stage only when they are ready for it.

Conclusion

As you go through the various activities in Section 2 and find techniques that you'd like to try with your next group, think of your programming repertoire as a continuum of techniques, not just as a grab bag of disconnected games and activities. Consider the extent to which each technique keeps control in the hands of the facilitator versus gives freedom to the participants.

Chiji Cards have traditionally been a processing tool to help individuals and groups talk about key moments in their experiences together. We also believe the cards can be used as a tool to help guide individuals and groups toward new key (or chiji) moments.

Our goal for this guidebook is to provide different ways for facilitators to use Chiji Cards for processing and group activities. Find the activities that work for you; change the ones that don't—and keep this truism in the back of your mind: "Do not be different to be different. Be good. If you are good, it will be different."

Activity Guide

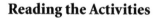

The activities in this guidebook take Chiji Processing Cards beyond their initial niche as a processing tool. Processing activities, of course, are included, but so are activities that frontload the action component of an experience, that provide object lessons to the action component, and that serve as the action component itself. Readers should feel free to adapt these activities for the best possible service to their programs' objectives. Utilize, explore, change, create, and have fun!

Reading the Activities

All 25 of the activities described in this book follow the same basic format, although not every subsection of the basic format appears in every activity. The subsections used throughout this guide are as follows:

Summary: This section provides a one- or two-line summary of the activity. It may also state explicitly the primary objective or predetermined outcome for the activity (also see the Appendix: Quick Activity Reference with summaries, p.106).

Needs & Numbers: This section contains the equipment you will need, as well as the ideal number of participants for the activity, based on our experience. The suggested number of people is kept relatively small, as it represents the number of participants who can actively participate in the activity. However, the activities presented in this guidebook may also work well with larger groups.

Time Line: This section approximates how long the activity will take. This, of course, may vary, depending on how engaged group members are in the process and how many follow-up questions are explored during discussion.

Setup: This section appears when some prior set up is needed. For example, it may tell you how to prepare or prearrange the Chiji Cards before the activity is presented—removing certain cards from the deck or putting cards in a specific order.

Directions: This section describes the steps of the activity. We have tried to offer complete instructions, but in some instances, directions may not address all of your concerns. If, after reading the instructions, you are left with questions, experiment on your own to work out the bugs. If, after that, you find that you need more information, or would like to share the results of your experiences with the activity, contact Chris Cavert at chris@fundoing.com.

Notes: This section is a must read. The notes contain supplemental information that helps facilitate that particular activity —thoughts, tips, cautions, and so on. If the activity becomes one that you use on a regular basis, make your own supplemental notes, keeping track of how the activity works best for you.

Follow-Up: This section includes possible discussion topics/questions that can follow the activity. **They are only suggestions.** Be open to other topics and issues that emerge from the group members as they work through the activity. Be careful not to get stuck in the mind-set of having to talk about predetermined subject matter. Be cognizant of the topics that are important to your group members; these are the things they will be interested in discussing.

Variation(s): Brief descriptions of variations of the original activity will be included in this section. Be sure to give them a look as one of the variations may be more appropriate for your program than the original activity. Develop your own variations. Consider writing them down and sharing them with others; please pass them along to chris@fundoing.com. Variations are to activities as spices are to food. If the food doesn't taste right, spice it up!

Chapter 1

Processing Activities

When an activity is completed and it is time to process, a facilitator may pull out his or her deck of Chiji Cards. The traditional way to use the cards is described in Activity #1 Picture Processing. To build upon the traditional use, this chapter includes five other ways to process with the cards.

#1 Picture Processing

The Traditional Use of Chiji Cards
Developed by Buzz Bocher, Dan Miller & Steven Simpson

The original way to use Chiji Cards is as a processing or debriefing tool immediately following an initiative or other experiential activity. The strengths of this original use are 1) it is easy for a facilitator to use, and 2) it involves a sharing circle so that every participant is gently invited to speak up.

Common rules of a sharing circle (form a circle and have each person share a thought):

- When it's a person's turn to speak, everyone else is quiet and gives that person full attention.

- "Pass" is an acceptable answer, although people are encouraged to speak if they have something that they feel comfortable telling everyone else.

Summary: Each participant chooses and shares one card that represents some aspect of the activity just completed. Picture Processing is designed so that every person makes at least one contribution to the facilitated discussion.

Needs & Numbers: One Chiji Deck is needed for a group of up to 15 participants, along with a comfortable and quiet area for discussion. If there are more than 15 participants, consider dividing the group in half and conducting concurrent sessions. Give each subgroup a complete deck of Chiji Cards or randomly split a single deck and give each subgroup half.

Time Line: 15 to 20 minutes—allow about 1 minute per participant.

Directions: Spread the cards, picture side up, and have the group sit around the cards so everyone can see them. Give the following instructions:

Each person pick a card that, for some reason, describes your feelings about the last activity. Choose carefully because, in about 60 seconds, I am going to ask you to name your card and explain why you chose that card. The feelings can be about you individually, the group, or the activity that we just finished. They can be about old feelings that this activity reminded you of. Take your choice seriously and give it a little thought. By the way, two or more people can choose the same card. If you and another person want to use the same card, move so you are sitting next to each other.

After all participants have picked their cards, group members take turns naming and explaining their chosen cards. Offer the opportunity to pass if someone is not ready or simply does not want to share his or her card with the group. Usually each person simply explains the metaphor derived from his or her card. If appropriate, ask pertinent follow-up questions. If you know the individuals in the group fairly well, try to steer them away from clichéd answers. For example, you might say something like, "Tom, you are always cheerful. I'm coming back to you in a minute or two, and I want more than 'I picked the sun card because I was cheerful during the last activity.' What else does the sun symbolize for you and this group?"

Follow-Up: In the above directions, participants were asked to choose a card that described their feelings. Obviously feelings are only one of many topics to process with the cards. The following are samples of other directions:

Choose a card that best represents a positive attribute that showed up during the activity.

Choose a card (or two) that best represents an attribute that did not show up during the activity—an attribute that would have been useful to the group had it shown up.

Choose a card that best represents the lesson of the last activity.

Choose a card that best summarizes the day [closing a day].

Choose a card that best represents something you learned today that you would like to use in the future [closing a day].

Variations: One of the potential weaknesses of the traditional use of Chiji Cards is that a dozen or more people answer the same question. The responses sometimes become redundant. Two ways to remedy this problem follow:

> **Variation 1/Pair Ups:** Have people in the group pair up and decide together on a card they both can relate to. Give pairs time to discuss the card they chose. Then, when each pair seems ready, have one person from the pair summarize their thoughts about the card with the whole group. This variation has two benefits: 1) if the group is large, it reduces the number of responses by half, and 2) the discussions that take place within the pairings as they decide which card to choose often enhance the quality of the answers.

> **Variation 2/Quartering:** Not everyone has to answer the same question within a single sharing circle. Depending on the size of the group, divide the circle into halves, thirds, or quarters. Then have each group respond to a different directive using the following instructions:

>> *Group 1, each person pick the card that best describes your feelings about the activity just completed. Each person in Group 2, pick a card that represents your individual contribution to the task. Group 3, choose the card that..., and Group 4, pick the card that....*

As you move around the circle to let people explain their cards, restate the question for that section. It has been our experience to have someone say, "I liked Section 2's question better than mine, so I answered that one instead." In most cases, this deviation from the stated instructions should be welcomed. If Section 2's question allows a person to say something that he or she needs to say, the sharing circle is working.

#2 Chiji Dyads

Developed by Bocher, Miller & Simpson

Chiji Dyads is an adaptation of the traditional use of Chiji Cards, so if you have not done so, familiarize yourself with Picture Processing (p. 14) before reading on.

Summary: Each participant chooses and shares one card that represents some aspect of the activity just completed. He or she discusses it with one other person from the group, and then with the group as a whole.

Needs & Numbers: One Chiji Deck is needed for a group of up to 16 participants, along with a comfortable and quiet area for discussion. If there are more than 16 participants, consider dividing the group in half and conducting concurrent sessions. Give each subgroup a complete deck of Chiji Cards, or randomly split a single deck and give each subgroup half.

Time Line: 15 to 20 minutes (allow about 5 minutes more than there are people in the group).

Directions: Have your group sit in a comfortable circle. Ask a specific question for the individuals in your group to answer with the card of their choice (e.g., What was your contribution to the group in the last activity? What are your feelings about how the last activity went? What card represents your view of the communication that took place during the activity?) Also, see Picture Processing for other possible questions.

Spread the cards, picture side up, in the center of the circle and give the following directions:

> *Each person pick one card that describes (insert your question). After you've chosen your card, find a partner and a*

P R O C E S S I N G — A C T I V I T I E S

spot away from the rest of the group where the two of you can talk. After everyone has a card, a partner, and a place to talk, I'll give you more directions. By the way, two people can have the same card. If two people pick the same card, then the two of you are partners. If three of you want the same card, then you become a group of three.

After participants have paired up and found a place to sit and talk, continue with the instructions:

Good. Now, explain your choice of cards to each other, but do it in a specific way. First, Partner No. 1 explains his or her card. Then Partner No. 2 asks one question about what was just said. Finally, Partner No. 1 answers the question. After the first card has been explained, reverse roles. Partner No. 2 explains his or her card, and Partner No. 1 asks one question. After both people have fully explained their cards, come back to the big circle.

The final step is for all participants to return to the single circle, where everyone is allowed to explain his or her card to the larger group. Ideally the dyads or small group discussions will have enhanced the quality of the big group card presentations.

Notes: As soon as you tell everyone to ask a question of his or her partner, someone might ask, "What kind of question?" You then must decide how much direction you want to provide. The reason for the question is to encourage people to think more deeply about their card, but you may want to keep the Q&A open ended. We suggest responding with something like the following:

Well, the purpose of the question is to help your partner explain herself or himself more clearly when we all get back together in a big group. Is there something about the explanation that doesn't make sense? Is there something about the explanation that seems superficial, but suggests something deeper? So, the idea is to ask a question that might help your partner understand his or her own card better.

Follow-Up: If a teachable moment presents itself, you could ask,

Was your explanation to your partner different from your explanation to the big group? If so, why?

How did the discussion with your partner clarify your thinking?

How did the discussion with your partner add to your understanding of your card?

Variation/Triads and Quads: Rather than dividing the group into pairs, divide it into larger groups of three, four, even five participants. Have one member of the group explain his or her card, followed by one of the others in the small group asking a question of the cardholder. Allow each person in the small group to explain his or her card and then answer a question. Before the small groups come back together as a single circle, give the following explanation:

When we come back together, it will not be necessary for each person to again explain his or her card. Instead, pick two memorable things that were talked about while you were in your small groups. It might be something that someone said when a card was explained. It might be something that came out of the discussion after someone explained his or her card. Identify two interesting things, pick someone to be the spokesperson for your group, and then come back to the big circle.

After everyone rejoins the big circle, let the spokesperson from each small group explain the group's two memorable things.

#3 Chiji Intuition

Developed by Cavert, Simpson, Miller & Bocher

Intuition will tell the thinking mind where to look next. —Jonas Salk

Summary: Participants choose a card at random and connect it to the activity just completed.

Needs & Numbers: A quiet place for a discussion and one deck of Chiji Cards works well for up to 15 players. If you have up to 25 players, use this activity as more of a self-reflection and don't have everyone share his or her thoughts with the group—some participants can just think about a particular card without sharing.

Time Line: 15 to 20 minutes—allow about 1 minute per participant.

Directions: After an activity is completed, spread the cards out—but put them **picture side down** so no one can see the images. Have the group members sit down around the cards. Each person chooses one card without seeing it. Depending on the group, decide how much you can play up that they are not just picking a card at random, but choosing the card that intuitively appeals to them. For example, you might say the following:

> *Please do not pick up a card yet. Has a waiter at a Chinese restaurant ever brought a tray of fortune cookies to your table and you knew which one was yours? Have you ever gone to a natural area to think a little bit and known intuitively which rock to sit on or which tree to sit under? For this activity, we are looking for that same kind of feeling. In about 15 seconds, I am going to ask you to choose one card. Try not to pick a card at random or just because it is the nearest card to you. Instead pick a card that speaks to you. Take your time—as much as a half a minute if that's what it takes. You may say, "I have to have that card" or, "They all seem the same to me," but give it a try. If two*

of you must have the same card, that's fine, you can share, but don't pick a card after it's been flipped over. Now calmly and slowly pick a card and place it face up in front of you.

Once everyone has a card and has placed it face up, continue:

Okay, I want you to think about what this card says to you about the activity that we just did. Take your time. In fact, we all will sit quietly for a full 30 (or 45 or 60) seconds. If you already know what the card represents, remain quiet so others can think. In a half minute, we'll go around the circle, and each of you can explain your card.

Allow participants to share their thoughts about the card they picked. If a player cannot come up with a connection (or chooses not to disclose the connection), he or she can simply pass.

Notes: Chiji Intuition sometimes works better than the traditional face-up use of the cards. Because cards are chosen blindly, the technique minimizes clichéd responses and forces participants to think about the relationship between the card and the experience. As an oracle process, the card is meant for the person who chose it—there is a message to be understood that might have meaning only to that person. Some people may think that the activity is silly, but there will also be participants who exclaim, "I cannot believe that I picked the _____ card! I'm getting goose bumps just thinking about it because...."

Follow-Up: If the group has done Picture Processing in the past and has just completed Chiji Intuition, ask it to compare the blind choosing of a card to choosing with the cards face up:

What did you like about choosing a card without looking at it? What didn't you like?

What did your mind go through as you tried to figure out the meaning of your card?

Was the meaning of the card better when you could see all of the cards or when they were all face down? Explain your answer.

Chiji Moments That Make You Say, "Hmmmm…"
Shared by Dan Creely

Ray Piagentini, the Illinois counselor of the year in 2007, invited Eugene to travel from Ireland to Illinois. Eugene came with the specific purpose of finding information on how to better serve the youth of his country who were at risk of suicide. He attended the first-ever Counselor Appreciation Series workshop on the topic of teen suicide hosted by the Illinois School Counselors Association in Lisle and the T.E.A.M. Conference at Northeastern Illinois University for guidance.*

During the T.E.A.M. Conference, Eugene was part of a workshop group facilitated by Ray. At one point in the program, Ray opened a new deck of Chiji Cards and spread them, picture side down, in the center of the group's circle. He set up a variation of Chiji Intuition with the declaration that participants would be choosing a card that would "speak" to them— a card that would tell them something they should pay attention to.

Near the end of the activity, Ray asked all the participants to turn over their cards so others could see them. Eugene smiled and commented to Ray, "I prefer to keep mine a secret until the end." His wish was honored. When Eugene finally revealed his card, it was the directions for using the Chiji Cards. Eugene smiled, and a quiet laugh moved through the group. The initial thought was that it was an error on Ray's part not to remove the directions card. But was it a mistake?

"In my haste," Ray said, "I did not remove the instruction card like I normally would, and as fate would have it, Eugene attended T.E.A.M. to get instructions for developing a suicide prevention program to take back to Ireland. This is one of those moments that make you say, 'Hmmmm… there's something more going on here than playing with a deck of cards.'"

* Teachers of Experiential and Adventure Methologies. For more information on these events, visit: www.ilschoolcouselor.org and www.neiu.edu/~team.

#4 Now & Then

Developed from *A Teachable Moment* by Cain, Cummings & Stanchfield

Summary: Individually or as a group, one card is chosen to signify what a person or group is feeling at the moment (i.e., immediately after an activity). A second card is chosen to signify what a person or group was feeling before the activity.

Needs & Numbers: A quiet place to talk and one deck of Chiji Cards works well with up to 15 people. If you have up to 25 people, run this one with the whole group at once, offering time for volunteers to share ideas about the two cards.

Time Line: 15 to 20 minutes—allow about 1 minute per participant.

Directions: Have your group sit in a comfortable circle. Spread the cards in the center of the circle, picture sides up. Ask each participant to choose two cards that best answer the "past and present" questions that follow. Have participants choose cards without actually picking them up, so it is easy for more than one person to use the same card or cards. Here are a few considerations to get the idea:

> **Individual Focus:** At the conclusion of an activity, say something like the following: *Look for a card that best represents how you are feeling since completing the last activity. Then identify another card that represents how you were feeling before the last activity began.*

> **Group Focus:** Say something like the following: *Think about the qualities of a team and decide on a card that best represents where you think your group is as a team after completing this*

last activity. Then decide on a card that represents where you think the group was as a team before beginning the last activity.

Once everyone has decided on two cards to discuss, allow some time for each person to share his or her thoughts. If you are working with a larger group, ask for ideas from some of the group members and then check in with others to see if they can agree on the cards that best represent the group now and then.

Notes: Now & Then can be presented in a number of different ways. Considering two cards together along with the idea of change is the basic concept. Also see The Catalyst (p. 66) for other ideas about looking at change.

Follow-Up: As your group moves through this processing activity, prompt participants to consider the reasons behind the change from the preactivity card to the postactivity card:

What type of change took place?

Can you recall the specific moment of the change and what inspired it?

Is this change something that could help in your everyday lives?

Variation 1/Now, Then & Later (from Simpson, Bocher, and Miller): The Now & Then concept also works well in one-on-one sessions. A facilitator or counselor can move through the following steps:

1) Spread out the Chiji Cards, picture side up.

2) Ask the participant to choose the card that best describes how he or she feels about him or herself today, and then allow the participant to explain that card.

3) Ask the participant to pick a second card, this one representing the way the participant felt about himself or herself at the beginning of the program. Again allow time for explanation.

4) Ask the participant to pick (and explain) a final card, representing how the participant wants to be at the completion of the program.

Once completed, the three cards represent a picture of the progress made and the distance yet to go.

Variation 2: There is no reason that the "before" card and the "after" card need to be picked at the same time. Before a group undertakes an activity, ask participants to choose a card that represents the group. Then, after the activity has been completed, give group members a chance to trade in their original card for a new one if so desired. To complete the trade, the participants need to explain why the switch is merited.

Variation 3: Frontload a program with Now & Then. For example, ask group members to decide on a card that best represents where they are overall as a team. (With some groups, it might not be possible to gain consensus on just one card. The group might end up with a few cards to describe where it is.) Next, ask participants to choose a card or cards that best represent where they would like to be, as a team, by the end of the program. Make a note of these cards and be sure to follow up at the end of the program to see where group members believe they ended up. What cards ultimately represented the group in the end?

When Do We Get to Ask the Questions?

#5

Developed by Steve Simpson's daughter, Clare, and her friends

The traditional use of Chiji Cards, as explained in Picture Processing (p. 14), calls for spreading out the cards and having the facilitator ask a question or two. A few years ago, Steve was using Chiji Cards with a small group of first graders, when one of the kids asked, "When is it our turn to ask the questions?" From the mouth of babes.... Even though Steve had been advocating for years that facilitators gradually turn the responsibility for processing over to the participants, it had never occurred to him to relinquish the ultimate power within a Q&A, allowing the participants to determine the questions.

Summary: Turn responsibility of asking the question over to the participants during the traditional use of Chiji Cards.

Needs & Numbers: One Chiji Deck is needed for a group of up to 15 people. Smaller groups of 5 to 10 participants work best.

Time Line: 10–20 minutes.

Directions: To set the stage for this activity, conduct one or two processing sessions in the traditional way of using the Chiji Cards (p. 14). Then say something like the following:

Now that you have a basic understanding of how to use Chiji Cards, let's take it a step further. It is easy to reflect on experiences when I am here to ask the questions, but I also want you to reflect or think about your actions when I'm not around. We will use the cards in the same way, but I'm not going to ask the questions. You are. Is there anyone who would like to ask a question of the rest of us?

Let one of the participants ask a question and have the other participants each choose a card that best answers the question. If several participants want to ask questions, do not have every person publicly explain his or her card. Have everyone choose a card, but allow enough time for only four or five participants to verbally explain their choices. The other participants will at least think about the card they chose, doing some personal reflection. For this activity, the questions tend to become more revealing than the answers.

Follow-Up: One good use of this activity is as a training course in asking good questions:

Why do you think it is worthwhile to let you ask the questions?

What makes for a good processing question?

Can there be a bad question? If so, what makes one question better than another?

Can anyone remember a situation when you were not with a teacher or leader but, after an activity, you asked yourself questions?

Variation: If you find it is important for all (or most) of the group members to share and ask questions, divide the larger group into four smaller groups. Give each group an equal number of Chiji Cards to work with. These processing quads can work together to ask and answer questions.

 **#6 Affirmation**

Developed by Dan Miller

Summary: Each group member chooses one card that represents a compliment to one other group member.

Needs & Numbers: One deck of Chiji Cards is needed for a group of up to 15 participants along with a short length of rope (24 to 48 inches) for each participant. If you don't have rope or string available, see Variation 1 for another idea. This activity works best with people who know each other fairly well.

Time Line: 15 to 20 minutes.

Directions: Give all group members a length of rope, asking them to hold one end of the rope in their left hand. Participants are then asked to offer the other end of their rope to a person who has been helpful to them. It can be related to some type of help received during the last activity or help received at any point during the entire day. However, each person can accept only one rope. In other words, the recipient accepts a rope with his or her right hand, and once that right hand has a rope, it cannot accept another rope.

Facilitators familiar with the initiative Human Knot will recognize that the group is now in position to play Human Knot.* The next step is for the group to untangle itself without letting go of the ropes. If the knot is twisted in a way that can be untangled to form a single circle, this is perfect. The group will create a circle where each participant is standing next the person he or she has been helped by. If the group ends up in a knot that cannot be untangled

---

* Wilderdom offers a good set of directions for Human Knot at http://wilderdom. com/games/descriptions/HumanKnot.html.

(or if the group ends up in two or more circles), let a connection or two be temporarily broken so that everyone ends up in a single circle. Once everyone is in a circle, participants may let go of the ropes and have a seat on the ground.

Put the Chiji Cards, picture side up, in the center of the circle. Say something like the following:

> *Each of you has chosen a person who has done you a service, a person you would like to thank—the person sitting to your left. Please pick the Chiji Card that best represents the compliment that you'd like to give this person. In about 30 seconds, we'll start sharing. Each of you in turn will present the card to your chosen person and tell all of us how this person has been helpful.*

After everyone has chosen a card, participants take turns presenting their compliment card to the person who was helpful to them.

Notes: Before presenting this activity, you'll want to feel confident that your group members will be able to share compliments with everyone in the group. In other words, do you think everyone in the group has earned a compliment? It might be awkward for those in the group who are left with giving a compliment to someone who has not done something to earn one.

Follow-Up: Sample questions follow:

> *How often do we compliment our colleagues?*
>
> *Were you comfortable publicly giving a compliment? Why or why not?*
>
> *How does the compliment that you received match up with the image that you have of yourself?*

Variation 1: If you don't have ropes, simply ask the group to circle up and sit down. Lay out the cards, picture side up, and ask everyone to pick a card that represents an affirmation for or compliment to the person on his or her right. Again, make sure that everyone in the group will be able/willing to provide a thoughtful affirmation for the person next to him or her.

Variation 2/A Human Knot: Rather than just handing the participants a length of rope, lay out the strands of rope on the floor like a big asterisk, with enough ends for everyone to have one rope end in each hand. Have participants circle around the ropes. Ask everyone to take the end of one rope in his or her left hand and the end of another rope in his or her right hand. Without anyone letting go of the rope ends, challenge the group to untangle the ropes in order to form a single circle. (It is possible for the knot to become too tangled to be undone, and sometimes the result of the group's work is two or more circles, but the idea is to create a single circle of people. Find a creative way to get the group into one circle if it doesn't end up that way.)

Once the group is in a single circle, proceed with the Affirmation activity, each participant complimenting the person to his or her immediate right. With this variation, the person who is to receive the compliment is somewhat random; only to be discovered once the ropes are untangled.

Chapter 2

Getting-To-Know-You

The activities in this chapter will help your group members get to know each other a little better. Chiji Cards have been commonly used to close an activity, but they can also be used to get things started. In most cases, these activities are delivered early in a program; however, don't let this notion stop you from adding them in when it feels right to do so.

Experiential educator Molly Foote of Bellingham, Washington, tells us, "The more we know about each other, the less likely we are to hurt one another."

 # #7 Chiji Connection

A variation of What You Say shared by Diane Phillips

Summary: Players mingle with the group, pairing and sharing with other players about what they have in common with the Chiji Card they are holding.

Needs & Numbers: One Chiji Deck for 10 to 48 players.

Time Line: Plays well for about 10 to 15 minutes.

Directions: After randomly dealing out a Chiji Card, picture side down, to each person, give the following directions:

> *Please mingle with the others and eventually pair up with another person. Introduce yourselves to each other and tell your partner what you have in common with the Chiji Card you are holding. If you absolutely cannot find anything in common with the card you have, simply say so. After each of you shares, exchange cards and consider how you are connected to this new card. Then introduce yourself to someone else in the group, and share your new card connection with him or her. If you can't immediately find a partner, raise your hand, look for someone else doing the same thing, and get together with this person. You have about 8 minutes to wander around and meet people. Don't forget to exchange cards before moving to the next person.*

Notes: If the participants seem engaged, let them continue with the activity. Also, the facilitator can be a participant in this activity. As a participant, you can better monitor the energy and sense when it is time to bring the activity to a close.

Follow-Up: Examples of questions that might be appropriate follow:

Without using anyone's name, did anything surprise you during the activity?

Did you find anything in common with some of the other players?

What made the activity challenging? What made it easy?

What would the activity be like without the cards?

What did the cards represent in the activity? What "cards" do you have in your lives that are helpful?

Variation 1: Have players take (up to 3) guesses as to what their partner's connection is with his or her card. If a correct guess cannot be made, the player holding the Chiji Card can share the commonality.

Variation 2: For more of a small-group exchange, divide your larger group into groups of 4 or 5 participants. Give each small group an equal number of Chiji Cards. Ask the groups to sit in a circle, placing their cards in one stack, picture side down, in the center of the circle. With this set up, have one person turn over the first card. Now, everyone in the group has the opportunity to tell the rest of the group how he or she connects to the card. After everyone has had an opportunity to share (people can pass if they don't see a connection), have someone turn over the next card and continue the process. Be sure to end the activity before any of the groups run out of cards to talk about.

Variation 3/Fact or Fable: Play Chiji Connection as directed with players mingling around with their cards. However, when people meet, they must state two connections with the card they are holding. One connection is a fact, the other is a fable (a connection with the card that is not true). Partners must then guess which connection is the fact.

For example a participant may say, "This is a ballot box card. It represents the fact that I worked for the Obama campaign in my hometown. It also represents that I was elected president of my junior class when I was in high school. Which one is the fact?"

#8 That Person Over There

Developed by Chris Cavert & Jim Cain

Summary: Holding on to one Chiji Card, players mingle around throughout the group, pointing out the person who originally chose the card they are holding.

Needs & Numbers: One Chiji Card deck is needed for a group of 15 to 35 players along with a midsize open space (away from the cards) for players to walk around comfortably.

Time Line: Plays well for about 15 to 20 minutes.

Setup: Set out all the Chiji Cards from one deck, picture side up, on a table or the floor, making sure all of the cards are visible to all of the participants. (Variation: Simply deal a card out at random to each player before starting.)

Directions: Ask everyone in the group to look over the cards and, within a 60-second time limit, pick up a card that represents a quality or characteristic he or she has. For example, one person might choose the clown because he likes to make people laugh. Another person might choose the painting because she is an artist at heart. For this activity, participants will not be allowed to share cards.

Once all the players have chosen a card, ask them to join you in the open area away from the cards. (If the extra cards are in the way, scoop them up and set them aside.)

At this point, ask the players to pair up with someone else in the group. (If there is an odd number of players, the facilitator could choose to join in the activity.) Tell everyone the following:

Every time you pair up with someone new in this game, please introduce yourself. If you already know the person, use his or her name along with a "hello." Now, after greeting your first partner, tell him or her about the quality or characteristic you share with the picture on your card. Be sure to really listen to your partner, because you are going to be passing along this information to the next person you meet. Okay, let's all go through this process with our first partner.

Give the pairs a little time to get through this first step. It shouldn't take too long; listen for the noise level to go down.

Has everyone had time to share?

Please, exchange cards with your partner.

When I say, "Go," begin mingling. Take your new card and move around the room with the intention of finding someone else in the group to talk with. If you need a partner, raise your hand, look for someone else doing the same thing, and get together with that person. First, introduce yourself or say "hello" using the person's name. Now, here's the new piece. Look around for that first person you spoke with, the one who has the quality or characteristic related to the picture on the card that you now hold. Point that person out to the new person you are now talking with, and tell this new person the name of the person who is connected to the card you are holding and the quality they share with the card. For example, if I have Sam's card and I'm talking to Sara, I will point out Sam to Sara and say, "Sam chose the eagle because he likes to go bird watching." Sara would then point out Anne, the first person she met, and say to me, "That person is Anne. She chose the frog because she likes to swim." Be sure you really listen to the information and look for the person being pointed out; you'll want to remember this information. Are you with me so far?

Take some time to clarify any confusion up to this point if needed, and then continue with the directions:

Now, here is one final piece before we continue playing. After you and your partner have pointed out to each other the persons connected to the cards you are holding, exchange cards with your new partner. Yes, you will want to remember who is connected to the new card you now have. At this point, go off to find someone else in the group to talk with. What's the first thing to do when you meet this new person? Yes, introduce yourself or say "hello." What's next? Each of you point out the person who is connected to the card you are holding, tell your new partner the person's name, and explain how he or she is connected to the card. After each of you explains connections, exchange cards and then move off to find another person to talk with. Continue this process until I call for a stop to the game. Do you have any questions?

After answering questions, give the group the "Go" signal. Play for about 5 or 6 minutes. If you play too long, like the game telephone, the information exchange could get stretched beyond recognition. Stop the activity with something like the following:

Okay, we're going to stop in about 10 seconds. Ten, 9, 8, 7, 6, 5, 4, 3, 2, 1, and freeze. Now, if all the information exchanging was clear, you should be able to go stand next to the person that was originally connected to the card that you are holding. When you find the person connected to the card, stand next to him or her and wait for my next directions. Ready? Go!

There will most likely be some extra work involved to connect players back to their cards. Some players may have lost some critical information along the way. In the end, it works itself out.

There are a couple of options as to how to conclude this activity:

Option 1: Give the following directions:

Now hand the card back to its original chooser, introduce yourself, and tell that person the quality he or she shares with the card. Is it the same quality the person originally shared? You might find some interesting surprises. Ready? Go!

Players will have to take turns sharing information, so there might be a little waiting—and that's okay.

Option 2: If working with a smaller group and time permits, interact with each person in the group. Starting with one person, here is a sample conversation:

Okay, let's see what you found out. What is the name of the person that is connected to the card you're holding?

It's Susana.

Okay group, who remembers how Susana is connected to the mountain card? [Encourage all the responses people remember, there might be more than one.]

[Back to the person holding the card.] *And what were you told the connection to the card was for Susana?*

Now, Susana, what did you say your connection to the card was? Interesting. Now, let's go to the next person....

From here, follow the same process for each person in the group. If the energy is good, move into some follow-up questions. Or, just let the group simmer in the fun and laughter that the sharing produces.

Notes: If you end up participating in the activity, be observant and listen to the group so you can determine if players understand the rules (do this during the transition times when connecting with a new partner). It's okay to stop the action and clarify, if needed. If you do not participate, mingle with the group and listen to some of the conversations in order to learn more about your group.

Follow-Up:

In your opinion, what was the most important part of this activity? Why do you think it's important?

Did anyone feel lost during the activity? Describe what "lost" meant to you? What did you do about it?

How would you describe the outcome of the activity? Why did it turn out this way?

What advice would you share with another group trying this activity, in order for that group to have a more accurate outcome of information?

What, if anything, did you learn about yourself during this activity that you might find useful later?

Variation: Go through the same process without the cards. This Chiji Card version of That Person Over There is a variation of the no-prop activity from the book, *The EMPTY Bag*, by Dick Hammond and Chris Cavert. Players simply share something about themselves with their first partner that is passed along. Using the Chiji Cards gives a useful visual reminder of the information.

If you really want to take this deeper, try the no-prop version first. Then, starting out with new partners, try the Chiji Card version. Compare the outcomes of each. What lessons can be learned from the comparison?

#9 Personal Stories

Shared by Dan Creely from Northeastern Illinois University

Summary: Used at different stages of a group's development, i.e., different times during a program, group members can learn a little more about each other.

Needs & Numbers: One deck of Chiji Cards can be used with a group of up to 25 people. Additional decks can open more opportunities for stories. A comfortable place for group members to sit is also needed.

Time Line: Provide about a minute for each group member to share a story and a few minutes initially to allow participants time to "find" a story they are willing to share. The activity will take a bit longer for a larger group. Another option is to divide into smaller groups, reducing the amount of time needed.

Setup: No prior setup is needed if the group is kept together for Personal Stories. If the group is divided into smaller groups (4 to 5 in each group is ideal), then divide your Chiji Cards equally among the groups.

Directions: This is the first of three possible levels for Personal Stories—the two additional levels follow.

Level 1: Have your group sit around the Chiji Cards that have been placed, picture side up, in the middle of the circle, making sure that each card is visible. Give the following directions:

Look over the Chiji Cards in the center of your circle and identify one that reminds you of a fun story from your past that you were a part of. Don't pick up the card just yet. You have about 2 minutes to find a story. When everyone has a story in mind, we will start. Each person will have about 1 minute to share.

After 2 minutes, continue with something like the following:

Okay, we will start your stories when I tell you to begin. Please stick to around 1 minute so we can stay focused and have time for some of the other activities we have planned. As always, if you don't want to share a story at this time, simply say, "pass." We'll come back to check in with you, as you might want to share later. When it is your turn to share, pick up the Chiji Card related to your story and hold it up for the group to see while you speak. During a person's story, the rest of us will be listening. When your story is over, place your card, picture side up, back into the center and say, "Thank you for listening." The rest of us will respond, "Thank you for sharing." Then the next person can pick up a card and share his or her story. We'll continue this process until everyone has had the opportunity to share. Are there any questions?

Have the group commence with the storytelling. If there are multiple groups, move around and listen to a story in each group. If appropriate, and time allows, share a story of your own. At the end, bring all of the smaller groups back together for some follow-up questions.

Notes: For logistical reasons, keeping track of the time during the activity is helpful. We initially give a couple minutes for quiet reflection as everyone looks over the cards, and then we start with the story time. When participants are getting close to the end of their 60 seconds, give a 10-second warning for them to finish their thoughts.

When there are multiple groups, provide the initial reflection time, asking everyone to stay quiet until story time starts. Then, encouraging each player to use his or her full 60 seconds, start the 1-minute rounds calling out the 10-second warning followed by a "switch storytellers" signal. Of course this works best if each group has the same number of people. Uneven groups may be off by a round, so have group members that have finished sharing personal stories spend the extra minute asking each other questions about their stories.

Follow-Up: To take the activity a bit further, ask a few questions about the experience. Keep in mind that it is not necessary to debrief or process each activity you present. An option would be to allow group members to ask each other questions about their stories. Sometimes, it's okay to move on and let the stories settle into those who heard them. Some ideas for discussion follow:

How many people learned something new about the people in your group? Why do you think this type of learning could be valuable?

What might be some advantages of sharing our stories? What might be some disadvantages of sharing our stories?

What qualities make up good listening?

Besides the actual content of the stories, what else did you learn about your group members?

Were you nervous about sharing your story? Where do you think this nervousness comes from?

Note: Level 2 and 3 options can be used after your group has worked together for a while, building a level of trust that can open up the space for more personal sharing.

Level 2: Ask group members to share a story about a memorable event they experienced in the past—something they feel comfortable telling the group. Using the term "memorable" opens the stories up to other aspects of a person's life, including scary moments, nostalgic memories, turning points, and challenges. Each group member will have his or her own comfort level.

Level 3: Ask group members to share a story involving a challenge they have gone through in their life. Here you are asking group members to be more specific about their stories. At this level, there should be a deeper level of connection within the group so people feel comfortable sharing. As always, each person has the opportunity to pass.

Variation/Level of Learning: This variation can be used at the beginning of a program to emphasize important learning moments in the participants' lives. Ask each group member to pick a card that tells a story about a memorable learning experience that he or she had. It might have occurred at school, with family or friends, or alone—any experience that, in retrospect, has made an impact on the way the person now thinks. Inevitably, many of the learning stories will be about hands-on experiences. Textbooks, lectures, and exams are rarely the things that stick in people's minds. After the participants tell their stories, the facilitator can frontload (without criticizing traditional education) the rest of the day by pointing out the role that experiential education already has in the participants' lives.

Chapter 3

Frontloading Activities

If Chiji Cards are an effective tool for making explicit the purpose of an activity after the experience has been completed, it makes sense they could also be used to accomplish the same task before an activity starts. The cards can serve as a way to introduce the action or some aspect of the upcoming activity. Such frontloading is making explicit, from the onset, the purpose of a specific activity or a day of activities. The idea behind frontloading is that if participants have an understanding of the expectations, objectives, and/or lessons of an activity or program beforehand, the follow-up debrief (or processing session) will be more clear and productive. The group or individual will have a better idea of what to talk about when the postaction processing takes place.

In most cases, facilitators set up activities just by telling a group what is about to happen. This straightforward approach is the most efficient way to convey introductory information quickly (e.g., goals, time frame, safety considerations), and it allows a group to get to the action component of an experience without delay. Still, a slower introduction to the action is sometimes appropriate, and frontloading activities are a way to make the introduction participatory. The following five activities are ways to frontload with Chiji Processing Cards.

#10 Chiji Representation

Developed by Bocher, Miller & Simpson

Summary: All members of the group choose one card that best represents their reason for attending your program.

Needs & Numbers: One Chiji Card deck is needed for a group of up to 15 participants along with a comfortable, quiet area for discussion. If there are more than 15 participants, consider dividing the group in half and conducting concurrent sessions. If you have two decks of cards, give each subgroup a full deck. If you have only one deck of Chiji Cards, randomly split the deck and give each subgroup half.

Time Line: Anywhere from 15 to 30 minutes depending on how the consensus building plays out.

Directions: Have your group sit in a circle on the floor (or ground). Scatter the Chiji Cards in the center of the circle so that all the pictures are visible. Present your group members with the task of identifying one card (or two) that best represents the reason they are attending the program. In other words, what card best represents why the group is there? The group must come to a consensus on one or, at most, two cards.

Depending on the group, you may have to define consensus as 100% agreement at some level. Every participant has veto power and is encouraged to use that veto power. If even one person doesn't accept the card in question, then the task is not complete. In consensus, the final card chosen probably will not be everyone's first choice, but it is a card that everyone agrees to accept. Differences of opinion, compromise, and give and take are part of the process.

Learn about your group members as they negotiate with each other toward a single card, and listen for the reasons people say they are there. You can also get a quick sense of the group dynamics. Who is adamantly campaigning for his or her first choice? Who is avoiding conflict? Who is actively seeking compromise? Who is engaged and who is not? The interaction between the participants in identifying their card may be just as important as the final result.

If your group is fairly large (i.e., more than 15 participants), divide it in half, and allow each subgroup to narrow its favorites down to two or three cards. When the subgroups come together, representatives from each small group must explain the rationale for their card choices to everyone else. Then the combined group members must narrow down the options from the cards available and settle on the single card (or two) that represents why they are there for the day. That card will probably be one of the cards chosen by one of the subgroups, but, if you leave all the cards from the deck visible, the group might decide on a "neutral" card that was not chosen by either of the smaller groups.

Notes: This activity does involve consensus building, which seldom occurs quickly. Be sure you can give the group ample time to complete the task. Having said this, there will be times when a group will not reach consensus. In the interest of time, there have been instances when we allowed groups to pick multiple cards or to move on without reaching consensus. Failing to reach consensus can be an excellent theme to carry forward into the main body of the program. At the end of the day, group members can be given a second chance to reach consensus as to why they attended the program together.

Follow-Up:

Why is it a good idea to know the reasons for attending a program like this?

How did people feel about the card selection process?

If some of you are not satisfied, how did the process fail to achieve true consensus? What can help you achieve consensus when you take on other challenges?

Who strongly argued for a particular card? Who was happy to compromise? Why did you take the approach that you did?

Did consensus lead to a good decision? What was good about it?

What was gained by using consensus? What was lost?

What else can your chosen card represent? How can we carry these traits forward throughout the day?

Variation 1: Start with a sharing circle (p. 14). Before asking the group to reach consensus, have each participant choose and briefly explain the one card that best represents why he or she came to the program. Participants don't need to pick up the card, just point it out when it's their turn to speak. Only after people have expressed their individual choices do you ask the group to work together to find a single card for everyone.

Variation 2/Name the Group: Rather than asking the participants to pick the card that represents their reason for being at the program, ask them to pick a card that will be the group's name for the day or for the week. A name may reflect their reason for being there, and additionally it provides a handle that can be used throughout the day. For example, the facilitator can ask, "Were you acting like Owls on the last activity?" or "Is this the level of cooperation that we've come to expect of Eagles?"

Excerpt from *Tips & Tools: The Art of Experiential Group Facilitation* by Jennifer Stanchfield

Using Chiji Cards can give groups an opportunity to create or find a symbol for their strengths and goals which can lead to group norms or "full value" agreements. I often used Chiji Cards with groups early on in their experience together to reflect. Later, when I engaged the groups in an activity to establish group norms, a particular Chiji picture naturally emerged as part of a symbol for the group. This happened in a profound way for one particular group I led in a 4-day facilitation skills workshop.

On day one, after presenting an early problem-solving initiative, the group chose the turtle card as it described their slow, deliberate, and thoughtful approach to the activity. Later that afternoon, I found out, one of the group members helped move a turtle across the road on her way home from the training. That same evening, I also discovered, another participant came upon a documentary about turtles as he was flipping channels back at the hotel room.

On the afternoon of the second day, when I asked group members to come up with a symbol to represent their strengths, goals, and commitment to each other, they went back to the Chiji deck and decided upon the turtle image once again. They drew their own turtle and decorated the shell with individual circles that represented each group member's strengths surrounded by the commitments to behavioral norms that would tie them together. They felt the turtle represented moving forward with their new ideas regarding facilitation in a slow and steady way. The group carried the symbol with it throughout the program and took a group picture with it at closing. These participants still refer to themselves as "the Turtles" when they communicate with me in e-mails or phone calls.

#11 **What Matters**

Developed by Hollace Bristol & Chris Cavert

Summary: The group decides on some of the important behaviors it would like to see take place during the program.

Needs & Numbers: One Chiji Deck is needed for a group of up to 15 people. If there are more than 15 participants, divide the group in half and conduct concurrent sessions. This activity works best if each subgroup has a complete Chiji Deck. Play out the activity with each group and then come together to share with the large group what was learned in the smaller groups.

Time Line: 20 to 30 minutes.

Directions: Divide participants into small groups of 3 or 4, and distribute the Chiji Cards evenly among the groups. Set the groups apart from each other like hours on a clock—a group at 12 o'clock high, another at 3 o'clock, 6 o'clock and so on. The idea is to place the groups so that all the small groups together form a larger circle.

This activity involves a number of rounds. For each round, the task is the same. Each small group's task is to choose one card from its possible choices that represents something it would like to see happen during the program—some type of action or behavior it deems important to the success of the overall group. For example, one small group might choose the clown to remember to have fun (this might also bring up the idea of clowning around and how that fits into the program). Another group might choose the parachute to encourage everyone to take risks because the group is there to provide support.

Set an exact time limit for choosing a card in each round (about 90 seconds), so every small group is ready to pass along its extra cards at the same time. When it is time, each small group will keep its chosen Chiji Card and pass the leftover cards from its initial set to the small group on its left, a counterclockwise path. Once each group has its new set of cards, the process starts again. With each consecutive round, the group sets aside another card. This overall process continues until the extra cards have made a complete rotation and each group has a chance to look at all of the cards (except for the cards that have been pulled out by the other groups). If there are time constraints, limit the number of times the extra cards are passed.

Once all the passes have been made and each group has its collection of chosen cards, the small groups reform to make a single large circle. Each small group presents the cards it chose and explains what its members would like to see take place. After each card is shared, ask if anyone else chose a card that has similar qualities—put these cards together to remember their connection. In the end, the attributes indicated by the combined collection of cards now represent the attitudes and behaviors, or norms, the group participants would like to see take place within the group as they work together. This norming process is an important stage in group development and should continue as the group grows and learns together. As the group changes, it will be important to reflect on, adapt, and change norms when needed.

Follow-Up: Throughout the course of the program, these cards (norms) can be revisited to assess how the group is doing. Some cards may turn out to be more useful than others. The group might notice norms come to light that were not identified by the cards. An option might be to choose a card that represents these new norms. The idea is to get group members thinking about how they want to be as they work together.

#12 Personal Strength

Suggested in _A Teachable Moment_ by Cain, Cummings & Stanchfield

Summary: Group members choose a card that best represents what they personally bring to the group in regard to behaviors and/or skills.

Needs & Numbers: One Chiji Deck is needed for a group of 15. If you have up to 25, divide into two smaller groups, giving each group half the deck. Play the activity with each group, allowing some time for individuals to talk before coming together as a large group and sharing.

Time Line: 15 to 20 minutes.

Directions: Spread the Chiji Cards, picture side up, on the floor. Have group members sit around the cards. Ask each person to identify one or two cards that represent behaviors or skills that he or she possesses that might help the group during its program.

After about a minute, ask group members if they have at least one card they are ready to share with the group (of course, every person has the right to "pass" on sharing). Have everyone willing to share talk about one card, then if you have the time, go around the sharing circle again and allow those who chose a second card another chance to speak.

Notes: It might be useful to keep a written record of what people share in order to refer to the list later. Information can be added or deleted from your list depending on the evolution of the group and its individual members.

The list of attributes could be used as prompts during the action component of the experience. For example, point out an attribute shared by someone in the group at a time when it would be useful, but is not being used. Such a nudge might encourage or remind participants to step up and utilize their stated talents.

Follow-Up: If you choose to discuss this frontload, you might ask the following:

Why is it important to know ahead of time what we all bring to this group experience?

How do you plan to remember what you all bring to the group?

Variation 1: If group members know each other well, and it is in line with the group's objectives, have participants choose cards for other people in the group. For example, highlight each person: "What does Susan bring to the group?" Then others in the group point to cards that relate to particular skills and behaviors she possesses. Use this variation selectively. The purpose is to bolster confidence, not tear it down. If you are not sure whether every group member will be complimented equally (because group members do not know each other well or because the group has a history of mean-spiritedness), do not use this variation.

Variation 2: Frank Palmisano Jr. shared this idea with us. Have group members pick a card that represents a strength or skill they bring to the group. Once each person has a card, everyone together tries to build a house of cards. Depending on the group, additional challenges can be added. Set it up so that the house of cards has to be a certain number of levels high (e.g., three levels) or be able to hold an object on the top of it, like a small stuffed animal.

If more cards are needed, allow group members to recognize more strengths and choose cards to match. Do a round with participants choosing a card for a personal strength and then choosing a card for a strength found in the person sitting next to them. Basically, try to point out that if participants are aware of and utilize their strengths, they can create a stronger foundation upon which to build. As the facilitator, ask group members if they think the strengths they are choosing are a good enough foundation for their group, or if there is more to offer.

Note for Variation 2: Be sure to guard against fabricating strengths in order to build a better house of cards—or maybe let the group suggest strengths they do not have, then discuss the topic after the experience.

#13 Focusing

Developed by Simpson, Bocher, Miller & Cavert

Summary: Chiji Cards can be used to help individuals and the group as a whole focus on a particular concept or idea they want to practice during an activity. Focusing is similar to Chiji Representation (p. 44), but as the name implies, its purpose is to focus the group even more toward a particular goal.

Needs & Numbers: One Chiji Deck is needed for groups of up to 15 participants along with a comfortable, quiet place to sit. With up to 25 players, simply open a conversation about what people want to focus on during the next activity as they look over the cards.

Time Line: 10 to 15 minutes.

Directions: Spread the cards on the floor or ground, picture side up. Choose the following options that best suits your group's needs.

Individual Focus: Ask participants to look for a card that "speaks" to them about something they want to work/improve on in the future—specifically, for the next activity as a result of participating in the previous activity. (Cards don't need to be picked up.) Once all participants have indicated they've made a choice, go around and let individuals point out or pick up their card and talk about the specific outcome they are after in the next activity. If they pick up the card, have them put it back so others can use the card.

Group Option 1: (Present this before you give the directions to your group's next activity.) Ask the group to choose, using consensus, a card that best represents a particular concept it wants to focus on as it moves forward, e.g., attributes that the group determines are important. For example, they may choose the light bulb to remember to take the opportunity to share ideas during the activity.

Group Option 2: (Present this frontloading activity after the directions to the next activity, when the group already understands the objectives of the upcoming activity.) Ask participants to choose a "focus" card that might help the group be successful in the next activity, as they understand it. For example, they might choose the ballot box as a focus to ensure they take time to hear everyone's voice during the process.

Once the cards are chosen and published (verbally shared) with the group, move into the next activity. Attach little sticky notes with the participants' names on them to the cards for reference during check-ins. Take some time during the activity to check in with participants or the group as a whole to see if they are, in fact, focusing on what they intended, or if something else is taking priority. Don't spend too much time during the activity, just enough to allow for a reminder. Spend the time you need during the follow up to go deeper.

Notes: Each of the options in Focusing considers an aspect of the future. If it's appropriate, this "future" could simply be stated in general as "some time in the future," or it could be related to a more specific time during your program. The difference is how and when the cards are used. Focusing group members **after** an activity helps carry something forward, whereas focusing **before** an activity helps the group think of something that might be important to bring into an activity.

Follow-Up: After the activity with the prefocus, check in with individuals or the group to see how their focusing was.

Did the chosen card(s) help you move through the activity?

Did the card(s) distract you? How so?

What helped you stay focused?

What distracted you from your focus?

What changed your focus?

Focusing Helps With Conflict Resolution
Excerpt from *Tips & Tools: The Art of Experiential Group Facilitation* by Jennifer Stanchfield

During graduate school I was facilitating a group of young adolescent boys who were part of a therapeutic group home program. This challenging group attended our program for 2 days. Day one of the low and high ropes course initiatives was successful. Throughout that first day the group engaged in a variety of reflective techniques including Chiji Cards. The boys were presented with the cards and each chose the symbol that best represented his role in the group.

When the group arrived on day two to participate in rappelling on our climbing tower, conflict was apparent. During some warm-up activities, they were not focused, made derogatory comments to each other, and exhibited behaviors that were not conducive to participating in the rappel tower. It seemed like we had taken several steps backward from the day before. I had to make a decision about my role as a facilitator that would affect the rest of the day.

I stopped the activity we were doing and asked the group to sit under a tree. I told them that we couldn't go on like this if they wanted to do the rappel tower, and that I was close to calling the bus to pick them up. I asked them to sit together for a while and make a decision about their participation as a group and figure out if they could or wanted to change. On a whim, I handed them the deck of Chiji Cards and said, "Maybe these will help."

About 10 minutes later, the other teachers and I came back to the group. The kids were seated in a circle under the tree; they were serious, focused, and attentive to each other. One student spoke for the group and stated that they had chosen the eagle card to represent their desire to "soar" on the rappel tower. He shared that they recognized that they were bringing each other "low" with their conflicts and that they needed to "rise above" their petty squabbling and soar on the rappel tower like eagles. They seemed sincere about this commitment, so we proceeded to the tower.

The boys were true to their words, and any time a group member demonstrated the slightest negative behavior, a peer would intervene immediately by asking, "Are you soaring?" It turned out to be a wonderfully successful day. The social workers that chaperoned the group were surprised and pleased. It was the first time they had witnessed the student who spoke for the group taking the lead and speaking during group process. The Chiji Cards helped this group move forward and focus on what its members wanted to achieve.

 **#14 Tool Kit**

This idea comes from *Survival: A Simulation Game* (available online at http://www.scoutingweb.com/scoutingweb/ SubPages/SurvivalGame.htm)

Summary: Group participants prioritize the 8 to 12 Chiji Cards that they believe will be good "tools" for the day.

Needs & Numbers: Ideally, one deck of Chiji Cards is needed for each group of 8 to 10 people. If you have multiple decks, give the same 8 to 12 Chiji Cards to each small group that is formed. If you have only one deck, photocopy the 8 to 12 cards you plan to use (see below) on a couple of 8½" x 11" sheets of paper, cut out the cards, and make the images available to each group.

Time Line: 20 to 30 minutes.

Setup: From the deck of Chiji Cards, choose the 8 to 10 cards that you think might best evoke ideas for a "tool kit" befitting your program and the objectives of the group (make your best guess as to the appropriate cards to use). For example, if the activity requires patience, you might include the turtle card because the turtle represents patience to you, which would be an asset for this particular group. It is important to point out that the activity will take longer if you provide more cards.

Even though you are narrowing the options, do not tell the group why you chose the cards you did—let the group determine their importance. Although the turtle card was chosen to symbolize patience, the group might think that card represents a hard shell, good swimming skills, or an ability to traverse on both land and water. The group's interpretation is as valid as yours, and you may not want to superimpose your values on the group. So, while you may select a dozen or so cards for specific reasons, keep those reasons to yourself. (Note that Chiji Cards intentionally have no text on them because the written word narrows possible interpretations.)

Directions: Divide your group into subgroups of about 8 to 10 participants. Give each subgroup its set of 8 to 10 cards with the following instructions:

We are going on an adventure today. Just like traveling into the wilderness or visiting a foreign country for the first time, you pack the things you think you will need—even though you are not sure exactly what you are about to encounter. The cards that you have symbolize things that you can take with you on today's adventure. The cards can represent, within reason, whatever you want them to represent. They might represent a physical object, an attitude that you want to have, or a skill that you think might be useful. Your job is to prioritize the cards as a group, lining them up from most to least important.

As the subgroups undertake the task, take the opportunity to mingle, observe, and listen in order to 1) learn what the groups most value, and 2) get a sense of the group dynamics within these small groups. After about 15 minutes, continue the instructions:

Now it is time for each small group to present its findings. Each card doesn't need to be explained, but I will ask you to tell the rest of us what your group considered to be the three most important cards and why they are at the top of your list.

Notes: The Wilderdom staff describes the steps for survival exercises in greater detail than we do here. For more information about using this kind of "survival" game, go to Wilderdom's Web site at http://wilderdom.com/games/descriptions/SurvivalScenarios.html.

Follow-Up: Follow-up can include asking for elaboration on the cards most valued (the top 3 or 4), as well as questions about the group dynamics in the decision-making process.

How did your group decide which cards were most important?

How did your group handle disagreements?

Who wielded the most influence and why?

What made this exercise difficult?

What were some memorable insights shared during the activity?

How did any of these insights influence the outcome?

What recent insights have been an important part of your lives?

Variation: The standard method for this activity is to preselect the 8 to 10 cards that you think are most evocative for the exercise. This variation works if you only have one deck of Chiji Cards and don't want to use photocopied game sheets. Randomly divide a Chiji Deck into piles of 12 cards and hand each of four groups one of the piles. You may not think a particular card has much significance, but that does not mean that participants won't find significance. After each group orders its cards, take the top three cards from each group. See if the larger group can order all the top picks.

Chapter 4

Object Lessons

From a current perspective, object lessons are facilitated discussions designed to address a specific issue. For example, the first object lesson, Obverse, reminds participants that even thoughtful and well-intentioned people can see the same thing in very different, sometimes opposing, ways.

Some readers will think that object lessons are just a form of processing or debriefing—processing with a very specific purpose in mind—and they would be right. An object lesson can be defined as a processing session with a specific purpose in mind. The distinction between processing activities and object lessons is that processing activities are associated with an action component, whereas object lessons can stand on their own. This is not to say that an object lesson cannot follow an activity, especially if the purpose of the object lesson coincides with an issue brought to light by that activity.

Object lessons can be one-shot discussions, but they can also be carried throughout a program or longer period of time. You might be able to reflect back to specific object lessons as the main idea of a lesson surfaces during other group activities. This, of course, reinforces the learning of the object lesson presented.

The following Chiji Card activities are facilitated discussions with very specific objectives.

OBJECT LESSONS

#15 Obverse

Adapted by Chris Cavert from the Michael Crichton book, *Travels*

Summary: Participants are given a chance to expand their willingness to see other viewpoints (i.e., the other side of the coin, the "obverse" side of things).

Needs & Numbers: One Chiji Deck is used for groups of up to 15 participants. If you have more than 15 people, divide into subgroups and give each group enough cards to work with—at least one card per person (one deck for each group is best).

Time Line: 15 to 20 minutes.

Directions: Spread out the Chiji Cards, picture side up, and have participants sit in a circle around the cards. There are a couple of presentation options.

> **Option 1:** Ask participants to look over all the cards. After consideration, each person is to pick up a card that he or she really DOES NOT like—a card that he or she thinks is a bad card. "Bad" will, of course, be defined by each person. In this particular activity, participants will not be able to share a card. Everyone should have his or her own individual card.
>
> Once everyone has a card, go through these questions one at a time, making sure everyone has an opportunity to answer the first question before moving to the second question.
>
> 1. *What do you think is bad about your card? (Or) What makes your card a bad card?*

2. *Now, think about and share something that could be
good about your card.
(Or) What might make your card a good card?*

Option 2: Ask participants to look over all the cards. After
consideration, each person is to pick up a card that he or she
really thinks is a "good" card—good according to his or her
own definition. Ask people not to share cards for this one.

Once everyone has a card, go through these questions one at a
time, making sure everyone has an opportunity to answer the
first question before moving to the second question.

1. *What is good about your card?
(Or) What makes your card a good card?*

2. *Now, what could be bad about your card?
(Or) What might make your card a bad card?*

Object Lesson: Here are some possible discussion questions to
bring out the object of this lesson:

What makes it possible to perceive things in more than one way?

What leads us to the way we see things?

*How can looking at something from a different point of view
change your situation?*

*What is something in your life that could change if you viewed it
differently?*

Notes: We like to use this object lesson near the beginning of a
program in order to consider how we perceive the new things
that might come up for people during the program. Some people
might find things boring or dumb, scary or risky. We can then
ask, "How might we look at this thing differently? What could be
fun about it, or what could be exciting instead of scary?"

When this activity was first considered, the setup was to choose
the "good" card first, followed by choosing the "bad" card. When

OBJECT LESSONS

we moved into choosing a "bad" card, the group knew what was coming so they put more consideration into choosing. This could work in your favor to emphasize the object lesson or it could be more than you need to get the lesson across.

We suggest using just one option (depending on the energy of the group) and bringing up the lesson when it presents itself during the program. For example, "How are you looking at the present situation? Could there be another way to look at it?"

Follow-Up: The object lesson itself might be enough to talk about, but here are a few other discussion ideas:

Is there some advice you might give to someone in the group about his or her card?

What did you think about before you chose a card?

What one card might help you change your perspective on something in your life right now?

Choose a good card you would give to someone else (within the group or outside the group). Who would you give it to and why?

Variation: After each person describes his or her "bad" card, ask someone else to explain why it may also be a good card. If handled in a nonconfrontational manner, participants appreciate the value of a different perspective.

#16 Relationships

Developed by Chris Cavert

Summary: The group works together to find cards that relate to each other.

Needs & Numbers: One Chiji Deck is used for groups of 2 to 15 players. This activity works better if every group has a full set of Chiji Cards so that all possible relationships can be discovered. If, however, you need to divide your group in half and have only one deck, 24 cards per group will work.

Time Line: 15 to 20 minutes.

Directions: Spread out the Chiji Cards, picture side up, and have participants sit in a circle around the cards. Ask the participants to look for pairs of cards they believe are related to each other. When someone in the group discovers a pair, he or she says out loud, "Relationship." Players do not immediately pick up the cards, but wait for the facilitator to give them permission to pick them up. This process does a couple things: First, if two or more players call "relationship" at the same time, the facilitator has the opportunity to determine the order in which the players will pick up their cards (this "management tool" can come in handy at times). Second, it prevents all the players from diving into and onto the cards.

Note: The way this is set up could also be a point of discussion for the group—the outside management of a process.

With permission, the player picks out the two cards in question and holds them up. At this point the player tells the group how the two cards are related. If everyone in the group agrees with the relationship, the group receives a point. If there is any disagreement about the relationship, a discussion can take place to try and determine how the group will decide on the pair. After the decision, the cards go back into the mix and other relationships are explored.

As the group's points increase, the relationships will end up being questioned even more. How the group works through this process is an important part of the activity.

Object Lesson: Here are some possible discussion questions to bring out the object of the lesson:

How do you define relationship? (What is a relationship?)

What are the factors that determine what a good relationship is and what a bad relationship is?

Who do you have relationships with in your life?

Share some details about one of your relationships.

Notes: We often play this by going around the circle, giving each person a chance to pick out a pair or pass. This keeps the process even more streamlined and orderly. However, we do like to use the random picking option when it is important for us to work on impulse control with groups. Going around in a circle helps us set up a structure that limits some behaviors.

Also, we have witnessed some pretty heated discussion where group members had a difficult time listening to each other. Be prepared to offer some skill development or training around healthy and productive discussion. You and your group might also have to establish some ground rules around how to determine the relationships.

Follow-Up: If it seems appropriate, follow up with these questions:

How did you feel about questioning other people's relationships?

Did anyone simply give in to a pair in order to get a point even though they questioned the validity of the relationship? Why did this happen?

How would you describe, using one word, the process that took place during a discussion about a relationship? How could any one of the discussions have been better?

If you could have an ideal discussion with your group that included some differences of opinion, what would the discussion look and sound like?

Follow-Up/After an Activity:

What relationship did you have with the last activity?

What relationships did the group support during the last activity?

Did anything strain any of the relationships you had during the last activity? If so, what were the strains?

What is important about relationships when working with a group?

Variation 1: Don't return the cards back to the mix. Ultimately, the game will end when the cards can no longer be matched or there are no cards remaining. The extra bonus challenge for the group could be to find a paired relationship for every card— ending up with 24 pairs that everyone agrees with.

Variation 2/Triads: There really is no reason to limit relationships to dyads. While it may not happen often, tell the group members that they can also choose matches of three, four, or more cards (see The Catalyst, p. 66).

 # #17 The Catalyst

Developed by the 2009 Indiana Teen Institute Group with Chris Cavert

Summary: The group is challenged to find three cards that have a particular relationship to one another. The first card is a starting point, the third card is an ending point, and the second card is a cause (or catalyst) for a change of some kind.

Needs & Numbers: One Chiji Deck is ideal for a group of up to 15 participants. If you have up to 25 players, keep everyone together.

Time Line: 20 to 25 minutes.

Directions: Spread out the Chiji Cards, picture side up, and have participants sit in a circle around the cards. This activity is similar to Relationships (p. 63). However, in this activity, group members are challenged to find three cards that fit together. The main idea is for the group to discover three (or four) card combinations that include a catalyst card that "precipitates an event."

For example: The combination of cards has a starting card (e.g., the farm card with the big blue sky and green fields) and an ending card (e.g., the cracked dirt card with the dead trees). Then there is a catalyst that is set between the two (e.g., the sun card, which caused the beautiful green field to dry up and the trees to die).

Have a player say the word, "Cards" when he or she has a three-card combination. Then, after receiving permission to pick up the cards, the player puts them down together for the group to see. If everyone agrees to the set, the group receives a point, and the cards are put back in the center along with the others. If the group does not agree on the set, the cards go back into the center without points (see Relationships, p. 63, for more on this process).

Adding another step to the activity helps participants look at it from a different angle: Have players (or the facilitator) call out "Catalyst" when they have chosen a middle card. After receiving permission, the player picks out his catalyst card and places it outside the mix of other cards. The rest of the group is then challenged to find the other two cards that belong on either side of the catalyst card. When a player calls out "Cards" and receives permission, he or she then picks up the two cards and sets them on either side of the catalyst. If these are the two cards the first player considered when choosing the catalyst, the group gets a point and then the cards are returned to the center and another catalyst can be chosen. If the two cards are not the ones first considered, the group could have a discussion about the fit. Do the cards work together or not? After the discussion, the two cards are returned to the center and another pair can be considered.

It might be good to establish a time limit when matching cards with the catalyst. We have seen some interesting combinations that might only be seen by the player who chose the catalyst. When the time is up, the player that chose the catalyst picks out the two cards that were initially considered to go with the catalyst card. The player then has the opportunity to explain the combination, and the group has the opportunity to discuss the rationalization. The bottom line is to have the group consider the concept of a catalyst.

Notes: If you have the time, it might be a good idea to hold a discussion about the group's understanding of the word catalyst. By pulling examples from various participants' personal experiences, the group can get a better understanding of how the activity will play out. This frontloaded conversation might address the object lesson in this activity as well.

For example, Chris' intention after high school was to become an Outward Bound instructor and spend his life in the woods. He did not have a very positive schooling experience growing up. After spending some time with his grandfather and visiting a local junior college, Chris decided to give it a try—besides, it was only two years. This college experience, where Chris was able to

OBJECT LESSONS

be in the company of exceptionally caring and engaging teachers, changed his life. He picked up the passion for lifelong learning. The catalyst, for what has been interpreted as a positive change, was Chris' grandfather.

Object Lesson: Here are some possible discussion questions to bring out the object of the lesson:

After playing this game, how would you define a catalyst?

What are catalysts that led you to something positive in your life?

What are catalysts that could lead you to something negative in your life?

How can the idea of a catalyst help you in this program today?

How can the idea of a catalyst help you in your life experiences outside of this program?

What type of catalyst could help you with something in your life at this time?

Follow-Up: If needed, ask questions like the following:

What was challenging about this activity?

If you could add a card to the deck, what would it be? How would this card help you in this activity?

How could this particular card help you in your life?

How could any other cards be a catalyst in your life right now?

Reflect on your last week of school (work, life) and tell us about a particular catalyst that showed up for you during that time.

What catalyst might have helped you during your most recent week in school (or work)?

Describe a time in the past that you have been a catalyst—either good or not so good.

How might you be more of a positive catalyst in the future?

Variation: Provide blank 3" x 5" index cards and markers. Let participants make their own catalyst cards to go with a pair of Chiji Cards.

#18 IWYRWWYG

(Is What You Really Want What You Get?)

Developed by Chris Cavert

Summary: With each group member choosing one card from a particular set of cards, participants learn about the concepts of conceding, compromising, and committing.

Needs & Numbers: One Chiji Card is needed for each participant in a group of up to 15 participants. One deck of cards will supply up to 3 groups of 15. We suggest having a facilitator with each group to guide the process.

Time Line: 15 to 20 minutes.

Setup: Take out enough Chiji Cards from the deck to equal the number of players in your group. For example, if there are 15 people in the group, choose 15 cards. It doesn't really matter which cards are chosen for the initial activity; however, keep the following in mind: Some cards tend to represent generally more positive concepts (e.g., the rainbow, the rose, the butterfly), and others tend to represent the negative (e.g., dry dessert, the lightning strike, the spider), while still other cards are more neutral (e.g., the railroad tracks, the globe, the lighthouse). Of course, your impression may not match those of your group, but some of the cards do represent commonly held, even archetypical, meanings. This activity tends to be more challenging when played with "negative" cards, so decide how deep you want the conversation to go and how much time you have to work on it.

Directions: Sit down in a circle with your group and lay out, picture side up, the cards you have chosen. Ask each participant to choose a card that represents something he or she wants. Tell participants not to touch the card they want or tell anyone else which one it is. (An option would be to ask participants to stay quiet during the time they are choosing a card.) Give the following instructions:

> *Think of this card as being very important to you. It could represent the next important step in your life. It could represent the job you're after. Maybe, once you have this card, you would know the secret of happiness. You really want this card. It is also important for you to know that, in the end, each card can only be picked up by one person. This means, to complete the activity, each person must have a different card from this set.*

After a minute or so, ask if everyone has the card in mind that they really want. If more time is needed, allow for up to another minute. Once everyone has chosen a card, one by one have the participants point to (and/or touch) the card they really want. For example, start with the oldest person or the one with the most seniority in the group and then continue around the circle.

If one or more cards are chosen by two or more participants, it is time for the group to work out a way for everyone to have a different card, but still get a card that is wanted. The level of facilitation you offer during this process will be up to the goals and objectives of the group.

Once all the participants in the group have decided on a different card, ask them to pick up their card and set it down in front of them. Before moving into the discussion (debrief), it might be helpful to ask again, even one person at a time, "Do you really want that card?" The way people answer might reveal more information to talk about and open the door to additional group work.

Consideration: The stated objective for IWYRWWYG is that each person should obtain a card he or she really wants from the cards provided. The facilitated objective is to explore the concepts of conceding, compromising, and committing. Once everyone has a card or the time runs out, move right into the follow-up questions to explore these concepts. If there is time, and the group appears interested, open a discussion about why each person chose the particular card they did. This discussion can often reveal a great deal about what people find important.

Notes: Wording for this activity is important. Using the word "need" instead of "want" can really change the dynamics of the process. Be very careful about how you talk to the group. Your suggestions might influence participants to make decisions based on pleasing you instead of going after what they want. If participants are fishing for help, simply say something like, "The objective is for everyone to end up with a different card—a card each person really wants."

Setting a time limit on this activity may be necessary due to the nature of some people's commitment to a card. If time runs out before the activity objective is met, consider adding some of the following questions to your follow-up:

How did the commitment to a card affect the activity? Is this good or bad? Why?

What are some negative outcomes that could occur due to a commitment to something only available to one person (e.g., starting quarterback, lead in a play, valedictorian, company manager)?

What are some positive outcomes that could occur?

Why were you so committed to your card? They are just cards after all.

Follow-Up: Before asking some of the follow-up questions, it might be necessary to talk about the concepts of conceding, compromising, and committing so that everyone in the group has a relatively similar understanding of each concept.

Note: Chris originally opened this activity with a discussion of conceding, compromising, and committing, but found over time that it worked better for him to talk about them once everyone had a card.

Ideas for questions follow:

What concept(s) did each person relate to during the activity?

When you saw someone else choose the card you wanted before it was your turn to choose, what did you do—concede (choose another card because it really didn't matter), compromise (choose another card because there was another one you really liked as well), or commit (stick with the same card)? Is this a typical response for you? Is it something you would like to change, and why?

What role did you play in the process if you ended up with a card that no one else chose right away? And, what is something you could have done during that time that you didn't think of right away?

What is good and bad (so to speak) about each of the concepts of conceding, compromising, and committing?

What are some examples in your life related to each concept?

Will you always get what you really want? Why? Why not?

Variation 1: Adding one or two extra cards to the set shortens the activity time.

Chapter 5

Initiative Activities

Although Chiji Cards were initially developed as a processing tool, they sometimes are used within the action component of the facilitated experience. Most notably, they can be used as the main prop for an initiative. Initiatives are activities that invite all group members to complete a given challenge, therefore requiring the group's initiative to accomplish a certain task. These activities can also initiate or bring about particular concepts such as trust, leadership, team building, and communication for the purpose of personal and/or group learning. The following are four simple initiatives using Chiji Cards.

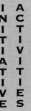

 # #19 Chiji Lineup

Traditional adventure-based activity—variation from Chris Cavert

Summary: The group members work together to line up in order, based on the Chiji Card each person has in his or her possession.

Needs & Numbers: A stopwatch and one Chiji deck is needed for a group of 8 to 12 participants (although this can be played with up to 48 people).

Time Line: 25 to 30 minutes.

Setup: Considering just one group of 12 participants for the moment, you will need to choose 12 Chiji Cards. The difficulty level of the activity will depend on the cards you choose. Initially, if you want to make it easy, choose cards from the deck that are easy to define (e.g., the lighthouse, the frog, the ballot box, the rainbow, the sun).

Directions: Give one Chiji Card to each group member. The group's goal is to line up, each person with card in hand, into alphabetical order based on how the card is named by the person holding it. When the group is ready, a "Go" starts the time. When the group is lined up in alphabetical order, the time stops. Check through the line to verify the "alphabeticalness" of the result.

After the group has set an initial time, and the expectations are clear, challenge the group members to improve their time. Before starting the next round, ask each participant to turn his or her card picture side down and then exchange cards with at least five other people (this is called a blind shuffle). Also give the group the option to plan between each round. When the group is ready, say "Go!" Stop the time when the group is lined up again. Check the result. After this second round, you and the group will have to decide whether to continue for an even better time or debrief the activity.

Consider starting out with an easier lineup (two or three attempts to get the best time) and then give the group members a more abstract set of cards and compare the process of the two different sets of cards. Questions follow:

How is it that the first set was easier than the second?

What needed to happen for the group to be successful with the second set of cards?

Why is this important?

Notes: One of the learning objectives of Chiji Lineup is the concept of mental models. Cards have to be defined—given a name—in order for them to be lined up alphabetically. So, how will the group come to agree on the name of each card as cards change hands? Initially, if the cards are fairly easy to define, the group will have little difficulty lining up after an exchange. However, how will the group handle more abstract cards like the broken pot, the bridge with the ducks, the comedy and tragedy masks, the cornucopia, or Father Time and Baby New Year? How will the group come to an understanding and agreement about the cards? It will take group work to reach the same mental model for each card. In this lies the lesson of mental models—how do we all come to agree on the same definitions or shared words?

Be ready for a number of solutions and problem-solving strategies in this one. Chris once used this activity with a group of college students. One of the students decided to name any card he ended up with an "absolutely awesome card," putting him at the front of the lineup. So, consider how much creativity you will allow.

INITIATIVE ACTIVITIES

Is it okay for participants to tell someone what's on the card they are handing another player during the blind shuffle? Depending on your program goals, set up expectations or roll with the challenges that present themselves. Allow the group time to sort out its plan. Options include giving them some planning time between rounds or forcing the group to ask for planning time by constantly pushing through to the next round. One of the main aspects of any initiative is to see what the group gets itself into and how the group is able to get out of it. This can involve some skill building through coaching or group discovery—it depends on your program goals.

Follow-Up: (Some of these questions are from the paragraphs above.)

Some names appear to be obvious, some are not, so how were you able to decide the name of the picture on the card?

How was the card name affected by the blind shuffle after each round?

Was there any group strategy to keep the cards' names unchanged?

How were the more abstract cards named? Did they change over time and why?

How did you come to understand and agree upon the names of the cards? What needed to happen for you to be successful with naming the more abstract cards? Why might this information be important?

How did you communicate with each other before, during, and after each round?

What did it take for you, as a group, to be successful?

What is important about the idea of mental models? How can this information help you at school/work?

Variation 1: If you want to try this activity with more than one group, simply put together a set of cards for each group—one card per person. There will not be enough cards to make all of the sets easy, so have a mix of easy and more abstract cards for each set. Or, if you are working on issues like privilege or diversity, intentionally give one group all easy cards and another group all difficult cards. Have a designated timer for each group and go three rounds. Or, set up a competition to see which groups comes in first, second, third…. Then, after three rounds, for an interesting dynamic, bring all the groups together to make one large community. Possible observations/questions follow:

> *How did each of you share what you knew in order for everyone to be successful?*

> *How did you communicate with each other before, during, and after each round?*

> *How does competition relate to cooperation?*

Variation 2: Some other possible card lineup concepts are 1) largest to smallest (defining the "size" of the card can be left up to the group or facilitator), 2) most powerful to least powerful, or 3) most important to least important.

Variation 3: Frank Palmisano Jr. shared this idea. After the group has created an alphabetical lineup of cards, have the group do a blind shuffle. Then, without talking, the players hold up their cards and then get into the correct order. The idea is to make sure everyone in the group knows the name of each card, or at least most of them, so they can help each other.

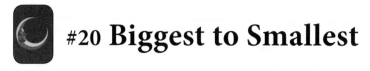 **#20 Biggest to Smallest**

Developed by Chris Cavert

Summary: As a group, come to consensus as to the order—biggest to smallest—of a particular set of cards.

Needs & Numbers: One Chiji Deck is needed for a group of up to 15 participants along with a comfortable place to work. If you have more than 15 participants, divide the group in half. Give each group the same time line and a different set of cards.

Time Line: 15 to 20 minutes (more time might be needed with multiple groups).

Setup: Before starting, create sets of cards for the group to work with. The more sets you create to put in order, the more time you will need for the activity. Also keep in mind that the number and abstract level of the card sets will affect the time needed for the activity. In most cases, fewer, less-abstract cards will take less time.

Note: If you choose to divide your larger group, ask the small groups not to share the way they ordered their cards with the other groups. After the initial round of ordering, switch sets of cards between small groups. See if there are any ordering differences between groups.

A unique aspect of this activity is that you can easily vary 1) the time that the activity takes and 2) the activity's level of difficulty. Compile several card sets, some easy and some more challenging, and then spontaneously pick and choose the cards sets most appropriate for your group. Stop presenting the sets when you see that your group has 1) met the facilitated objectives of the activity, 2) met the appropriate level of challenge, or 3) used the allotted amount of time for the activity.

Here are a number of set examples, listed in less to more challenging (relatively speaking) order. The cards within the sets are not listed in any particular order. So, how would you place them in biggest-to-smallest order?

- the moon, the farm scene, the globe (earth), the sun
- the keyhole, the teepee, the globe (earth), the ballot box, the rose, the rock bluffs
- the frog, the bee, the rabbit, the spider, the owl, the turtle, the ostrich, the butterfly
- the train tracks, the safe, the clown, the fire, the light bulb, the cornucopia, the wind, the rainbow, the eagle, the sunset

Directions: Gather your group around a table or sit on the floor. Spread out the first set of cards, face up, so all the players can see all of the cards. Simply say, "By consensus, place these cards in order from biggest to smallest. When you have reached your solution—one that everyone can agree on—let me know." Give participants time to work out their solution.

When the group is ready for another set of cards, present the cards in the same way as the previous set. Move through as many sets as you believe to be appropriate for your group.

Notes: This might be a reasonable activity to teach your group about consensus building by starting with small sets of cards (providing some initial success) and then progressing to more challenging orders and more abstract cards. Be sure your group has some knowledge of the process of, and tools for, consensus building, and then use this activity to practice the concept.

Follow-Up: Here are some possible questions to explore during or after this activity:

On a scale of 1 to 5—5 being very challenging—how challenging was each set to get into an order you all agreed on? What made each set less or more challenging?

INITIATIVE ACTIVITIES

How are some of these challenges like the ones in your own life? What can you take from the challenges here into your own day-to-day experiences?

How do/did each of you define biggest and smallest?

Consider presenting more questions about mental models and the pros and cons of seeing things differently. Then ask, "How do we complete a task when people see things differently?" This can go into conceding, compromising, and committing issues (see IWYR-WWYG on p. 69 for more on the three C's).

Other possible discussion topics could include how the group's consensus process went, how the communication was, and if leadership played any part in completing the activity.

Variation: Show individual cards to all members of the group in order to determine if the people in the group believe the image on the card is BIG or small. For example, sit in front of the group, hold up a card, and ask, "In your mind, is the image on this card big or small?" Then, go around the group and find out where people are with each card. The probing question for this is, "In relation to what?" Explore what this means. When someone determines something, what is it in relation to? Connect this to real life. A person thinks someone is a bad dresser—in relation to what? Someone is having a bad day—in relation to what or whom? In other words, what do other people's bad days look like? A seemingly bad day might not be so bad.

#21 Card Trains

Developed by Chris Cavert

Summary: In this puzzle challenge, the group puts as many card trains together as possible, connecting the end of one word given to a card to the beginning of another word given to another card.

Needs & Numbers: One Chiji Deck is needed for a group of up to 15 players. Provide a full deck of cards for every group of up to 15 players in order for everyone to have hands-on contact with the cards. Open working space is needed to lay out the card trains.

Time Line: 15 to 25 minutes (depending on how the activity is presented).

Directions: We consider Card Trains to be a puzzle challenge for groups. Some learning styles are really drawn to puzzles. The initial challenge is to connect as many cards together as possible, with a minimum of three cards in each train. A follow-up challenge is to make the longest possible train, maybe even challenge the group to try to use all the cards in the deck. If you do present the extra challenges, we suggest that you set a time limit.

Each card can have a number of words associated with it. For example, there is a card with a dried up dirt scene with two dead trees. Card words can include dirt, trees, dead, horizon, branch, dry, and barren. Interpretations are numerous, but everyone in the group must agree to the given word for each card—consensus building.

To continue with the dead tree card example, let's use "dirt." Now, the next task is to find a word in another card that starts with the last letter of the initial chosen word (dirt), which, of course, is "t." There are some train tracks in the deck. The group could use "track" or "tracks," but they opt for tracks so that they can link it to the spider card. They pull out the spider card followed by a rain cloud. The group's first train of four cards is complete. (Interestingly enough, these four words make a "word circle" since "cloud" reconnects with "dirt"—but this is another topic, and a train would not go very far if you hooked up the beginning of the train with the end... we digress... sorry. Anyway...)

So, readdressing the objective, the group's challenge is to connect cards together in trains of at least three cards and, at most, all the cards (we've never seen this yet, but some day...). Once a train of three or more is made, another train can be started. Groups can make trains of any size between these two numbers.

Before starting on the challenge, assess your group to determine what it needs. If necessary, set up a process for picking up cards to avoid aggressive grabbing; keep the process manageable. Do you want to work on consensus building by requiring that all card train connections be accepted by all the members of the group (see Biggest to Smallest on p. 78 for more practice with consensus building)?

Notes: There are two aspects of this activity we've found to be very interesting and useful. The first is the progression or parts of the activity that always seem to evolve. Initially, there are questions to determine if the words the players are coming up with are acceptable to the facilitator—boundaries are being explored. Then there is a flurry of work, often done by a particular group of people with a few others just watching the process. Gradually, the work starts to slow down when most of the cards are connected. Then the people who were quietly watching start to come forward and fit in the unlinked cards, as well as rearrange some of the cards already on the table in order to make more of them fit. Some of the fast-and-furious workers, at this point, start to check out of the process. This tends to be a great example of how a group often functions together—lots of great things to talk about.

The second aspect of this activity involves collaboration. During a task, a large group often fragments into smaller pods of people, resulting in the resources (cards) being segregated from the whole. In our experience, if the small pods don't come together at some point in the process, more cards will be left at the end. If the pods open up, they find they can use and integrate more cards in the process—again, so much to talk about.

Follow-Up: Consider the following questions:

In relation to how your group communicated during the activity, how would you rate the group on a scale of 1 to 10, 1 being very poor, 10 being excellent?

How were the usable words on the cards chosen?

Who knew the usable words on the cards?

Did everyone in the group agree to all the card train connections? How do you know?

Describe how you saw, heard, or felt the activity progress. What were the different "parts" in the activity, and what do you find to be important about each part?

Did any of you find yourself checking out of (not participating in) the activity? When and why do you think you checked out?

As a group, on a scale of 1 to 10, how would you rate your success with this activity? What were some of the key factors to your success? How could your group move up just one point on the success scale?

Variation: To emphasize the objective of everyone being on the same page, randomly quiz people on the Card Train connections once the group has indicated it is done. The idea is to be sure everyone in the group knows the information (the card connections) related to the task.

INITIATIVE ACTIVITIES

#22 Four in a Row

Cavert & Sikes, variation of Word Builder in *50 More Ways to Use Your Noodle*

Summary: Each small group is challenged to acquire four cards that go together, helping the group understand that cooperation can be more productive and more amiable than competition.

Needs & Numbers: Using one deck of Chiji Cards, this plays well with 8 to 28 players. You will also need a long activity rope or cones to outline a large area—about 20 feet by 20 feet.

Time Line: 15 to 30 minutes.

Setup: Create a circle boundary area that is about 20 feet in diameter using the activity rope. If you only have cones to mark the corners, make the boundary area a square that is 20 feet by 20 feet. Be sure all the players understand where the boundaries lie.

Place all the Chiji Cards, face down, inside the boundary area, spreading them out away from each other so that no one card is touching another card. Call this inside space the card area. Call the space outside the boundary lines the home area.

Directions: (To fully understand this activity, read Card Trains on p. 81 before continuing.) Once the set-up is complete, divide your large group into at least 3 but no more than 7 smaller groups. For example, a group of 28 players could be 7 groups of 4 people, 20 players can be split into 5 groups of 4 people, a group of 8 can become 4 groups of 2 players each. Ask each small group to find a place in the home area that it will use as its home base. This selected area is where each group will build its Four in a Row.

The four cards in a row will be formed in exactly the same way as in the activity Card Trains. If it fits into your program, have the group play Card Trains at some point before it plays Four in a Row. This will give group members an idea of how the cards fit together. If you don't play Card Trains, take time to explain the process of how the cards connect. FYI: We don't let our groups use colors in the cards—too many distractions. But, it's up to you.

Each small group's objective is to put together four cards that are connected in some way. Here is a possible step-by-step presentation to make to the group:

- *Players gather at their group's home base.*

- *The objective is for each small group to connect four cards together as described in Card Trains.* (Replace this directive with instructions if they have not played Card Trains.)

- *One person from each group is allowed into the card area to retrieve one card at a time.*

- *The person picking up the card, and the rest of this person's group, may not look at the card until the person who picked the card is back at the group's home base.*

- *If the group decides to keep the card, place it on the ground, picture side up, at the group's home base, and another person from that group can enter the card area to pick up another card.*

- *If the group decides not to keep a card at its home base, another person from the group returns the card to the card area, placing it picture side down. Then this person chooses another card to bring back to the group for consideration— remembering not to look at the card until it is back at the group's home base.*

- *Cards may not be taken from another group's home base.*

- *No more than four cards can be at any group's home base at any one time.*

- *When a group achieves Four in a Row, its members together yell, "Done!" A facilitator then will check the work.*
- *Finally, this activity is not over until every small group has four cards in a row that make a verifiable connection.*

Ask the groups if they have any questions. When everyone is ready, let them begin. To reiterate, the activity is not over until each small group has four cards in a row.

Notes: Here's the facilitated objective of the activity. When small groups are done putting their four cards together, is the activity over? No, not until each small group has four in a row. So, when the first small group has its four in a row, what do they do? Do they stand around? Do these players cause distractions for others still playing? Do any of the players find a way—following the rules—to help other groups? Herein lies the lesson.

It is common for everyone else to stop when one group finishes, assuming that the activity is over. (FYI: At any point during the presentation was the word "team" used?) At this point, it is up to the facilitator to remind the groups that the activity isn't over until every group has four cards in a row. Be careful not to say much more. It is not facilitation if you tell the groups to help each other. This is for the group, as a whole, to discover. Let the groups play it out. If players ask if they can help other groups, simply say, "Is that breaking any of the rules?" or "It's up to you."

Follow-Up: Here are some questions to consider asking once the group is finished with the activity:

Was the activity set up as a competition? Did the activity feel competitive to you? Why?

Was there a winner? What would the rest of the players be considered?

What did it feel like to be the last group to get four in a row?

Did anyone have an idea of helping other groups? What did you do with the idea?

What was the activity like when all groups were on their own?

What would the activity have been like if helping occurred?

What was the activity like when helping occurred?

Did your small group want help?

How did your small group react to other people helping?

At any time did you think the rules were being broken? In what way did you think the rules were being broken?

What is something to remember about this activity?

Variation 1: A way to encourage group think around helping is to time the activity. Start the time when the activity begins, and stop the time when the last group gets its four in a row. Then challenge the group to brainstorm ideas about how to get a better time. In most cases, helping behaviors are discovered.

Variation 2: The activity is a little bit easier if you let each group have up to five cards at home base, still building a train of only four cards.

To be playful and serious at the same time is possible, in fact, it defines the ideal mental condition.
—**John Dewey**

Chapter 6

Fun With Chiji Cards

Fun is an important factor in any type of group programming. Steve Butler (1995), in the book *Quicksilver*, reminds us, "When the fun disappears, people's energy and enthusiasm are often next" (p. 13). We hope our groups will have fun with the activities we have planned and, at the same time, discover some of the educational aspects inherent in each one. However, there are times when you just want to have some F.U.N.N. as Karl Rohnke says— Functional Understanding Not Necessary. When programming this type of fun(n), the primary goal is not to explore the learning or function of the activity, but to enjoy the experience of it. It's also just good to take a break from thinking every now and then.

Here are a few "funn"-fillers using Chiji Cards.

#23 What's On My Card

A variation of a traditional guessing game

Summary: Each player is challenged to find out what is on his or her card by asking others in the group "yes" or "no" questions.

Needs & Numbers: You'll need a room-size, open area and a deck of Chiji Cards for up to 25 players. You could play with as many as 48 since there are 48 cards in the deck; however, some of the cards are really tough to guess.

Time Line: 10 to 15 minutes.

Setup: Before getting started it will be important to consider the difficulty level of the game. There are approximately 33 Chiji Cards that are pretty easy to define (i.e., fire, frog, rainbow, light-house, light bulb). There are approximately 15 pretty abstract cards that are more difficult to define (i.e., comedy and tragedy masks, the silhouette of a person with birds flying in it, Father Time and Baby New Year, the ostrich with its head in the sand). For this description, let's keep it easy. Pick out enough of the easy cards so each person in your group has one.

Directions: Deal out a card, picture side down, to everyone in the group, and ask players not to look at their cards. Facilitators can play too as long as they don't look at their cards! If a player accidentally sees his or her card, have the person exchange with another person in the group (as long as this person didn't see the card either).

Here's the objective. When signaled to start, everyone with a card holds it up to his or her forehead with the picture facing out. By doing this, everyone except the person holding the card can see it. Participants now mingle throughout the group, asking other participants "yes" or "no" questions in order to find out what is on the cards they are holding. For example, "Am I something in nature?" "Am I alive?" "Could I be found in a school?" "Am I an animal?" "Can I carry this in my pocket?"

To get players to talk to more people, tell them they can only ask one question at a time of any one player. They must ask at least one other person in the group a question before coming back to someone they've already talked with.

When a player finds out what's on the card, he or she hoists the card in the air and proclaims, "I found out what's on my card!" At this point, the player no longer needs to hold the card on his or her forehead. However, players who know their cards can continue to mingle, letting other players ask them questions.

Notes: We suggest setting a time limit on this activity since this game might prove to be more challenging for some than others, depending on the card they have. Frontloading this activity might be an option, saying something like, "Some of you might not be able to find out what is on your card until you look at it. This is okay. Simply do the best you can to ask questions that might help you solve the challenge."

Variation: For some groups, allow players to help each other with hints. Give a few examples of what constitutes a reasonable hint. Challenge everyone to try to find out what is on his or her card without using hints, but allow participants to ask for help when they feel they need it.

#24 Telling Stories

Summary: The two activities included below involve telling stories using the Chiji Cards as prompts.

Needs & Numbers: One deck of Chiji Cards works well with up to 15 players. If possible, use chairs for Story Activity 2: Circle Story.

Time Line: 10 to 15 minutes.

Story Activity 1: Deal a Story (a variation of the traditional Build a Story activity)

Directions: Play this one around a table or sitting on the floor. Deal out all the cards to your group, dealing yourself in as well, if you wish. This means that, depending upon the size of the group, each player may have 2, 3, 4, or more cards. Players can look at their cards as soon as they get them.

To start the game, say something like, "Once upon a time…" or "It was a bright sunny day on planet Tah, when…." This opens the game for any player to use one of his or her cards to begin the story.

This is how it works: If any of the players have a card they believe will work in the story (or to start the story), this person calls out, "Card!" If only one player calls it, the facilitator gives permission for the player to state a sentence that fits into the story. If more than one player calls out "card," the facilitator choses a person to play. The player then contributes to the plot of the story using the image on the card as part of the story. Once a player states his or her sentence and lays down the card picture side up, another player is open to call out "card" and add to the story.

The challenge for each story is to have every player contribute at least one story line to the narrative. This might take some people playing two cards before another player uses even one card. If time allows, collect, shuffle, and deal the cards out again for another story.

Notes: This activity is about fun creative expression. The stories can be as wide open as you allow (we like to keep them G-rated).

Variation: After a warm-up round or two of dealing all the cards out, present the group with the "one-card challenge." Shuffle and deal out one card to each player. Start with, "Once upon a time…" and see if the group can create a logical story with everyone adding his or her card to the story at some point.

Story Activity 2: Circle Story (a unique variation from Jim Cain)

Setup: Set up a circle of chairs facing out, one fewer chair than the number of participants, i.e., in the same way that a game of musical chairs is set. Game spots arranged in a large circle about two feet apart work as well.

Directions: Have each player randomly choose a Chiji Card from the deck and then sit down in one of the chairs (or stand on a spot)—everyone facing away from the center of the circle. When we lead this activity, we have a facilitator take the first turn as storyteller to demonstrate the action. The storyteller does not need a card and does not have a chair (or game spot). Ask the players to hold up their cards in front of them so the storyteller can see the pictures clearly. The storyteller starts, like all good storytellers do, with the opening, "Once upon a time," and then starts to walk around the outside of the circle. He or she then adds to the story featuring particular cards being held up by the players in the circle.

For example, "Once upon a time, I was driving by a farm and I saw an eagle flying overhead." When the farm card and eagle card are called, the players holding those cards get up and follow the storyteller around the circle.

The story might continue, "When I stopped to pick up the clown that was hitchhiking, a lizard crossed the road in front of me. Now, the players holding the clown and lizard cards join the parade around the circle.

And the story goes on, "Once we started moving again, we noticed the beautiful sunset off to the west. It was a good trip… The end!" On the words, "The end," everyone in the parade (the storyteller and those following) is required to find a seat—sitting down carefully into the chairs! The player left without a seat is the next storyteller.

Before the new story begins, the cards that the players are holding can be collected and new cards handed out, or the new storyteller can simply hand over his or her card to the player without one (the previous storyteller). Once everyone sitting down has a card, the new story can begin. "Once upon a time…."

Notes: Stress safety issues when using chairs. A body tumbling over with a chair could be a game-stopper. Ask the people still sitting in chairs when "The end" is called to spot the players getting into the chairs.

Variation: If you want to mix things up a bit, allow the storyteller to use any variation of the word "change" (i.e., change, changing, changed) in his or her story. When one of these change variations is used, everyone sitting down must leave his or her seat, travel in the direction of the hand holding the card (if a player is holding the card in his left hand, he must travel to the left), and then sit down in another empty chair that is not directly to his or her right or left. Players must move at least two seats over. As soon as the storyteller is able, he or she continues moving around the circle telling the story.

#25 Group Concentration

Traditional game adapted by Simpson, Bocher & Miller

Summary: The group is challenged to match up all the cards available as quickly as possible.

Needs & Numbers: Two decks of Chiji Cards are needed for this one. This activity plays best on a flat surface like the floor or a table with up to 12 players. With up to 24 players, divide the group in half and give each group 12 pairs to uncover (24 cards). Use a stopwatch to time both groups together, either for an overall group effort or for a head-to-head competition.

Setup: Put together 12 pairs of cards and set the extra cards aside. After shuffling the 24 cards, set them out in a four-by-six-card grid with the picture sides down.

Directions: The challenge is for the group to match all the cards as fast as possible. (It plays like the old concentration game using traditional playing cards.) Players, one at a time, take turns flipping over two cards. If the cards match, the pair is taken out and the next player takes his or her turn. If the cards don't match, both cards are flipped back over, picture side down, and the next player takes his or her turn. The rest of the group can offer advice to the player taking the turn; however, only the player whose turn it is can touch any of the cards.

Before starting, have the group establish a turn order. Each player is required to take one turn flipping over two cards before anyone can take a second turn. After giving the group some planning time (if needed), begin the activity and start the clock. When all the cards are matched up, stop the clock. If time allows, play another round to see if the group can beat its best time.

Variation: If you are under a time constraint, change the goal to see how many pairs the group can match in 5, 8, or 10 minutes. To make the activity a bit longer, add more paired cards to the initial set up (e.g., five-by-six-card grid for 15 pairs, or six-by-six-card grid for 18 pairs).

Chiji Cards
Closing Activity Variations

The activities described in this book were designed as specific educational exercises. The point that we are making here with the closing activity variations is that some of the activities in this guidebook that were used early or midway in a program can also be used to close out an entire day or program. This section provides variations of the activities presented earlier that can be used to wrap up a group experience. Instead of including the complete activity description here, we ask that you return to the original activity description, keeping the suggested closing variation in mind.

Picture Processing (p. 14)

At the end of your program, spread the cards out, picture side up, in the center of the group's circle. Ask each person to choose a card that represents his or her overall connection or feeling about the program or extended program experience. Players do not need to pick up the card from the center until it's their turn to speak. After sharing, the card can be put back into the center for others to use if needed. Depending on the time frame, consider limiting each person's sharing experience to under 1 minute. If we are closing an extended program (more than 1 day), we like to leave a fair amount of time at the end in order for people to share without being limited to a minute.

Chiji Intuition (p. 20)

At the end of your program, spread the cards out, picture side down, in the center of your group's circle. Ask everyone in the group to take a minute to scan over the cards. When participants are ready, they can choose a card, placing it picture side up in front of them. After some reflection time over their card, participants share thoughts about how their card connects them to the program (or maybe what this card is saying to each person about what to consider for the future—what is the card telling them?). Participants can think of this like a fortune cookie. What message is in it for them? Consider allowing participants to take their card with them if an important connection is made.

Now & Then (p. 23)
Spread out all the cards, picture side up, in the center of the circle, and simply change the language of the individual and group focus:

Individual Focus: Say something like, *Look for a card that best represents the idea or thought you had about this program before you arrived and a card that best represents your idea about this program now that you have gone through it.*

Group Focus: Say: *Think about the qualities of a team* [or any other aspect of the group's program], *and decide on a card that best represents where you think your group is as a team after completing this program. Then decide on a card that represents where you think the group was as a team before beginning the program.*

If appropriate, add, *Choose a third card that best represents where you want to be as a group in the future.*

After some time to reflect, allow group members to share their thoughts.

Personal Stories (p. 39)
This is a slight variation of Picture Processing. Spread out the cards in the center of the circle, picture side up, and ask players to consider a few cards (up to three cards) that tell a story about the person's experience in the program.

We often explain, *Use up to three cards to help you craft a story that you can tell others about your program experience. Each of you, in turn, will then reach in for the cards you need for your story. After telling the story, return the cards to the center for others to use.*

Chiji Representation (p. 44)

Give the same directions as in the frontloading activity, but ask the participants to choose a card, through consensus, that best summarizes what they learned from the program. In retrospect, the original lessons might be clearer; they might even be different. When appropriate, use Chiji Representation twice with the same group, once as an opening and once as a closing. The results might reveal some interesting changes in perspective.

Focusing (p. 53)

The Chiji Cards are spread out, picture side up, in the center of the circle. Participants decide on a card that speaks to them about something they want to focus on as they move back into their everyday lives. After some reflection time, allow people to share their aspirations. When possible, let the participants take home the card they chose as a reminder of their goals.

 **Chiji Cards**
Tips & Twists

Some of the best learning opportunities with Chiji Cards come from taking advantage of a special moment when the cards are being used in a conventional way. Almost without thinking, we add a small twist or let an unusual digression run its course, and the result exceeds our expectations. Sometimes the teachable moment is so unique that it cannot be replicated. Other times, however, it can be. By just making a small change in delivery, we can create a setting where the likelihood of a special moment is increased.

The following is a list of tips and twists for getting even more from the Chiji Cards. These ideas come from experiences that we and others have encountered while exploring Chiji moments.

1. There have been particular times when we **let participants keep their cards**. Most participants are not going to find strong attachment to an image on a card, but every once in a while, someone is deeply touched by a particular card. For whatever reason, the card takes on personal meaning. At that point, it makes good sense to give the card to the person to keep. Your deck will work just fine with a missing card or two. If you give away a half dozen cards over a course of a year, be thrilled that your program is making such impacts on people, then break down and buy a new deck, keeping your old deck for additional giveaways.

2. If the group chooses or focuses on a particular card, **use the card to represent or identify the group**. For example, "Okay, you Eagles, let's get together in a circle," or "How would the Eagles deal with this problem?" or "Instead of

calling it a sharing circle, how do you feel about calling it an Eagle's Nest?"

3. **Use Chiji Cards selectively.** We use all of the activities in this book, but seldom do we use more than two or three of them with any particular group. We do not want to use the cards so often that participants start rolling their eyes when the cards come out. An exception might be when we have the same group for an extended period of time. Both of us, for example, are university teachers, so we have the same students for an entire semester. In that situation, we may use Chiji Cards up to a half-dozen times over a three-month period, and familiarity with the cards actually contributes to the continuity of the course.

4. **Substitute other prompts for Chiji Cards.** If you want to use several of the activities from this book, but not overwhelm participants with repeated Chiji sessions, use another tool in place of Chiji Cards. Author and experiential educator Jennifer Stanchfield of www.experientialtools.com uses postcards, charms and other small objects, and catch-phrase buttons in the same way that she uses Chiji Cards. Michelle Cummings of Training Wheels, www.training-wheels.com, uses plastic body parts (eye, ear, hand, heart, etc.). One educator at a workshop told us that he uses the front panels from breakfast cereal boxes, creating an extra-large set of picture processing cards.

5. If you journal in your programs, **Chiji Cards are great prompts for free writing** and reflective contemplation, either during or away from the program.

6. **Casually leave the Chiji Cards laying around.** If you have a group for an extended period of time, especially if there is a fair amount of down time, have your deck of Chiji Cards out for participants to pick up (e.g., when a cook group on a backpacking trip is preparing dinner and those not in the cook group are just sitting around). Don't push the group to use the cards; don't even mention that the cards are available. Simply

set them out where they might be noticed. Occasionally a handful of participants will spread out the cards and process or play on their own.

7. **Use Chiji Cards to help your larger group get into smaller groups.** Be sure everyone in your group is holding on to a card (this happens easily after activities like Chiji Connection and Chiji Lineup). Simply ask everyone to get into groups of 4 or 5 by finding a relationship or connection throughout the cards they are holding. Challenge the group with, "all the cards have to have something in common," or, "there could be a linear connection where one card relates to one other card, this other card relates to another card, and so on down the line." We've done this to create pairs as well. Once everyone is in the smaller groups, you're ready for the next activity.

8. By design, the Chiji Cards do not have words on them. However, a number of our facilitator friends **utilize the space on the back side (nonpicture side) of each card** for some additional contemplation. Using a permanent marker, they wrote words, energizing phrases, even short quotes, to use as another reflection tool with their groups. One facilitator told Chris, "When I did this with my cards, I didn't choose words that connected to the picture on the other side—I didn't set out on purpose to do this. However, by accident, some participants ended up making a connection. That's why I love this field. You just never know what's going to happen."

9. Are you a geocacher? (See www.geocaching.com.) **Chiji Cards can be a great treasure to leave behind in caches.** Here's an idea. Get a set of cards and number them on the nonpicture side as a set like this: 1 of 48, 2 of 48, 3 of 48... up to 48 of 48. Then start leaving the cards during your geocaching adventures. You never know who will start collecting them or reflecting on their meaning. If you laminate a favorite card, you could send it out as a travel bug. Punch a hole in one of the corners in order to attach the tag. Where will you want to send one for a visit?

10. For some spontaneous fun, Frank Palmisano Jr. uses the **Chiji Cards for charades**. He shares, "You might need to presort the cards to get appropriate ones, e.g., eagle, turtle, ostrich, owl, the painting, and so on. One member of the group would pick a card at random and have to act it out for the group to guess. This fun, energizing game could start to touch on [and open up discussions about] nonverbal communication." Keep in mind that the fear of standing up in front of others can make charades a high-risk activity for some people.

11. **Laminate** the Chiji Cards, especially if they are going to be used in the backcountry. Use the thinner lamination sheets (3 mm) if you have a choice. After the plastic cools down, trim the extra laminate from the edges of each card, cutting right up to edge of all four sides of each card. The deck will be thicker after the lamination, so find a container other than the original box. A small zip-type plastic bag works well.

 # Epilogue

More than most books, this is a work in progress. Some readers will read through the activities listed here and exclaim, "Hey, they didn't even describe my favorite way to use Chiji Cards." Other readers will try an activity in the book and immediately discover a slightly better way to facilitate it. Throughout the book, Chris has asked readers to send comments to chris@fundoing.com. We make that invitation one more time.

Some of your comments might show up on the Wood 'N' Barnes Publishing Web site, www.woodnbarnes.com, in the Friday Lessons. We might even be able to add a couple of activities to a revised edition of this book at some future date. We started this book by stating that experiential educators are tinkerers. As such, the activities in this book are not finished products. They are serious drafts of programming ideas that might fit well into your educational adventures. Chris likes to think of them as kindling to those experiential fires. So now, we encourage you to use this kindling and get your own fires started.

The activity was symbolic, a metaphor for life. It was a right-brain experience that would stick in the unconscious and conscious mind forever.

—Unknown

Appendix: Quick Activity Reference

Activity	Page	Summary	Number of People
#1 Picture Processing: Traditional Use of Chiji Card	14	Each participant chooses and shares one card that represents some aspect of the activity just completed. Every person can make at least one contribution to the facilitated discussion.	up to 15 or divide group
#2 Chiji Dyads	17	Each participant chooses one card that represents some aspect of an activity just completed, sharing it with one other person from the group, then with the whole group.	up to 16 or divide group
#3 Chiji Intuition	20	Participants choose a random card and connect it to the activity.	up to 15*
#4 Now & Then	23	Individually or as a group, one card is chosen to signify what the person/group is feeling immediately after an activity. A second card is chosen to signify what the person/group was feeling before the activity.	up to 15*
#5 When Do We Get to Ask the Questions?	26	Turn responsibility of asking the question(s) over to the participants during the traditional use of Chiji Cards.	up to 15
#6 Affirmation	28	Each group member chooses one card that represents a compliment to one other group member.	up to 15
#7 Chiji Connection	32	Players mingle with the group, pairing and sharing with other players about what they have in common with the Chiji Card they are holding.	10 to 48
#8 That Person Over There	34	Holding on to one Chiji Card, players mingle around throughout the group, pointing out the person who originally chose the card they are holding.	15 to 35
#9 Personal Stories	39	Used at different stages of a group's development—different times during a program—group members can learn a little more about each other.	up to 25

Chapter 1: Processing Activities

Chapter 2: Getting-To-Know-You

* variation provided for up to 25

2010 © Wood 'N' Barnes Publishing, Bethany, OK, 800-678-0621

Appendix: Quick Activity Reference (continued)

	Activity	Page	Summary	Number of People
Chapter 3: Frontloading Activities	#10 Chiji Representation	44	All members of the group choose one card that best represents their reason for attending your program.	up to 15 or divide group
	#11 What Matters	48	The group decides on some of the important behaviors it would like to see take place during the program.	up to 15 or divide group
	#12 Personal Strength	50	Group members choose a card that best represents what they personally bring to the group in regard to behaviors and/or skills.	up to 15 or divide group
	#13 Focusing	53	Individuals and the group as a whole focus on a particular concept or idea they want to practice during an activity.	up to 15*
	#14 Tool Kit	56	Group participants prioritize the 8 to 12 Chiji Cards that they believe will be good "tools" for the day.	8 to 10 per deck*
Chapter 4: Object Lessons	#15 Obverse	60	Participants are given a chance to expand their willingness to see other viewpoints.	up to 15 or divide group
	#16 Relationships	63	The group works together to find cards that relate to each other.	up to 15 per deck
	#17 The Catalyst	66	The group is challenged to find three cards that have a particular relationship to one another. The first card is a starting point, the third card is an ending point, and the second card is a cause (or catalyst) for a change of some kind.	up to 15*
	#18 IWYRWWYG	69	With each group member choosing one card from a particular set of cards, participants learn about the concepts of conceding, compromising, and committing.	up to 45

* variation provided for up to 25

2010 © Wood 'N' Barnes Publishing, Bethany, OK, 800-678-0621

	Activity	Page	Summary	Number of People
Chapter 5: Initiative Activities	#19 Chiji Lineup	74	Group members work together to line up in order, based on the Chiji Card each person has in his or her possession.	up to 48
	#20 Biggest to Smallest	78	As a group, come to consensus as to the order—biggest to smallest—of a particular set of cards.	up to 15 or divide group
	#21 Card Trains	81	In this puzzle challenge, the group puts as many card trains together as possible, connecting the end of one word given to a card to the beginning of another word given to another card.	15 per deck
	#22 Four in a Row	84	Each small group is challenged to acquire four cards that go together, helping the group understand that cooperation can be more productive and more amiable than competition.	8 to 28
Chapter 6: Fun With Chiji Cards	#23 What's On My Card	90	Each player is challenged to find out what is on his or her card by asking others in the group "yes" or "no" questions.	up to 25 per deck
	#24 Telling Stories	92	Two storytelling activities using the Chiji Cards as prompts.	up to 15
	#25 Group Concentration	95	The group is challenged to match up all the cards available as quickly as possible. (Needs 2 decks of Chiji Cards.)	up to 12 or up to 24 (2 decks)

References & Resources

The following is a limited list related to processing and debriefing. A couple of the references (i.e., Cain, et al. and Sugerman, et al.) focus on instructions for specific processing activities. The others emphasize theory and/or general practice.

Bacon, S. (1983). *The conscious use of metaphor in Outward Bound.* Denver: Colorado Outward Bound School.

Boud, D., Keogh, R., & Walker, D. (Eds.). (1985). *Reflection: Turning experience into learning.* New York: Nichols Publishing.

Cain, J., Cummings, M., & Stanchfield, J. (2005). *A teachable moment: A facilitator's guide to activities for processing, debriefing, reviewing and reflection.* Dubuque, IA: Kendall Hunt.

Gass, M. (Ed.). (1993). *Adventure therapy: Therapeutic applications of adventure programming.* Dubuque, IA: Kendall/Hunt.

Greenaway, R. Active reviewing guide to facilitating reflection, debriefing, and transfer. http://www.reviewing.co.uk (a comprehensive source of debriefing tools).

Hammel, H. (1986). How to design a debriefing session. *Journal of Experiential Education, 9(3),* 20–25.

James, T. (1980). *Can the mountains speak for themselves?* Retrieved from http://www.wilderdom.com/facilitation/Mountains.html

Joplin, L. (1981). On defining experiential education. *Journal of Experiential Education, 4(1),* 17–20.

Knapp, C. (1992). *Lasting lessons: A teacher's guide to reflecting on experience.* Charleston, WV: ERIC Clearinghouse on Rural Education and Small Schools.

Luckner, J. L., & Nadler, R. S. (1997). *Processing the experience: Strategies to enhance and generalize learning, 2nd edition.* Dubuque, IA: Kendall/Hunt.

Priest, S., Gass, M., & Gillis, L. (2003). *The essential elements of facilitation.* Dubuque, IA: Kendall/Hunt.

Quinsland, L. K., & Van Ginkel, A. (1984). How to process experience. *Journal of Experiential Education, 7(2),* 8–13.

Rohnke, K., & Butler, S. (1995). *Quicksilver: Adventure games, initiative problems, trust activities and a guide to effective leadership.* Dubuque, IA: Kendall/Hunt.

Simpson, S., Bocher, B., & Miller, D. (n.d.). Chiji Processing Cards information and instruction sheet.

Simpson, S., Miller, D., & Bocher, B. (2006). *The processing pinnacle: An educator's guide to better processing.* Bethany, OK: Wood 'N' Barnes Publishing.

Stanchfield, J. (2008). *Tips & tools: The art of experiential group facilitation.* Bethany, OK: Wood 'N' Barnes Publishing.

Sugerman, D. A., Doherty, K. L., Garvey, D. E., & Gass, M. A. (1999). *Reflective learning: Theory and practice.* Dubuque, IA: Kendall/Hunt.

 **About the Authors**

Chris Cavert, Ed.D., is an internationally known speaker, trainer, and author in the area of Adventure-Based Experiential Activity programming. He focuses on using adventure education to develop prosocial, community-building skills within groups of all ages. Chris' educational doctorate is in the area of curriculum and instruction with a focus on adventure education. He also holds a master's degree in experiential education and is the author and developer  of over a dozen adventure-based education publications and products. You can e-mail chris@fundoing.com and visit Chris at: www.fundoing.com.

 **Steven Simpson, Ph.D.,** is a professor in the Department of Recreation Management and Therapeutic Recreation at the University of Wisconsin-La Crosse. He also has taught at National Taiwan University and National Taiwan Normal University. Along with Buzz Bocher and Dan Miller, he co-created Chiji Processing Cards. Steve can be reached at simpson.stev@uwlax.edu or chijiorders@chiji.com.

Many vendors of experiential education books and products supply Chiji Processing Cards, including:

Wood 'N' Barnes Publishing & Distribution
2309 N. Willow Avenue, Suite A
Bethany, OK 73008
800-678-0621
info@woodnbarnes.com
www.woodnbarnes.com

Institute for Experiential Education
115 Fifth Avenue South, Suite 503
La Crosse, WI 54601
608-784-0789
chijiorders@chiji.com
www.chiji.com